CAROL... Writing...es

IDEAS, EXERCISES, AND ENCOU...
FOR TEACHERS AND WRITERS OF ALL AGES

ILLUSTRATED BY ROB SHEPPERSON

Stenhouse Publishers
Portland, Maine

For Peggy Laufer, Alice Shea, Mark Hardy, Anna Cantelmo,
Liz Charpentier, and for all teachers everywhere, with love
and thanks for the great work you do

Stenhouse Publishers
www.stenhouse.com

Library of Congress Cataloging-in-Publication Data
Coman, Carolyn.
    Writing stories : ideas, exercises, and encouragement for teachers and writers of all ages / Carolyn Coman ; illustrated by Rob Shepperson.
        p. cm.
    ISBN 978-1-57110-871-5 (pbk. : alk. paper)—ISBN 978-1-57110-917-0 (eBook)
    1. Language arts (Elementary). 2. Creative writing—Study and teaching. 3. English language—Study and teaching. I. Shepperson, Rob. II. Title.
    LB1576.C57757 2011
    808—dc22

                                                                        2011007002

Cover, interior design, and typesetting by Martha Drury
Manufactured in the United States of America

PRINTED ON 30% PCW
RECYCLED PAPER

17 16 15 14 13 12 11   9 8 7 6 5 4 3 2 1

CONTENTS

ACKNOWLEDGMENTS

Stenhouse is a terrific publisher. Many people there helped me—with such kindness and professionalism—to make this book what it is. Thanks to Chris Downey and Jay Kilburn for overseeing the production, Andre Barnett for her careful copyediting, and Martha Drury for design. Thanks to Nate Butler, Dan Tobin, Zsofia McMullin, Rebecca Eaton, Chandra Lowe, and Chuck Lerch for their marketing expertise and guidance. Jennifer Allen and Maureen Barbieri read messy drafts of this book, and their insightful reports helped me enormously to make it better. Rob Shepperson's drawings enrich the text, and collaborating with Rob enriches my life.

Toby Gordon, true editor and true friend—thanks for *everything*.

INTRODUCTION

*T*hank you for giving this book a try. My intention in writing it is to be of use to you—writing teachers, teachers who write or want to write, classroom teachers, mentors, and intermediate, middle school, and high school teachers—and through you, to be of use to your students.

I do not have a set curriculum to offer or a foolproof technique or program. (I don't even *believe* in such things when it comes to writing.) I'll leave grade-by-grade reading lists and annotated bibliographies to those far more qualified to compile them than I. What I do have are thoughts about writing stories, from having written a bunch of them for children and young adults, and ideas about teaching, from having taught writers of all ages. These days I teach mostly adults—emerging writers who write stories for children. But I've taught in plenty of classrooms over the years, and I promise you this: when it comes to talking about stories and writing, I say essentially the same things to writers of any age, whether they're five or eighty, whether they're teachers or students.

Millions of words have been written about writing and the writing process, and I truly hesitate to add one more syllable to the heap. What could possibly be left to say? Honestly, nothing. But as I often remind my students about story writing, no one ever says the same thing in the same way. My editor, Toby Gordon, believes I have helpful things to say to teachers and to their students, and I've learned over the years that if you are lucky enough to find a wise and true editor, you should listen to her (or him), and so here I am. I'll use the same approach in writing this book that I use in writing stories and novels—working toward simplicity and clarity to get to the core of the matter.

For me, story is core. It is the only way I know to talk about writing and to teach writing. Basically, I see most communication as some version of or variation on telling a story, whether it's fiction or nonfiction, a book report, a speech, a college entrance essay, or a science or history paper (what *is* history if not a collection of stories?). Helping your students understand and incorporate the shape of a story—its beginning, middle, and end—will make them stronger writers in any genre or form. Having them practice, over time, saying what they mean with chosen words sequenced in an order that makes sense and aimed toward a larger understanding will translate across any subject matter. Inviting them to value and consider their thoughts, dreams, curiosities, and experiences will serve them well in everything they do.

Focusing on writing stories may seem like a luxury you think you can't afford. However, I truly believe that whatever time and energy you devote to teaching your children to write good, clear, solid stories will pay off in many ways, in many disciplines, for everyone.

For years I taught a fiction-writing workshop at Harvard Extension. During the semester, we isolated and concentrated on basic elements of story—character, plot, voice and dialogue, setting, and so forth—before students began writing and revising their own short stories. This book takes the same basic approach, focusing on specific aspects of story and writing and including exercises that I and my students have used.

I realize that not everyone is in a position to give sustained attention to story writing for a period of weeks or months. Everything in this book can be adjusted. Over the years, I have adapted, shortened, or lengthened my lessons and exercises to suit a wide range of audiences, ages, and writing levels, for semester-long classes, day- and weeklong workshops, and one-on-one mentoring. I encourage you to do the same: pluck from what I have to say as you see fit, making whatever adjustments and variations work best for you and your students. There are no sacred cows, and nothing is written in stone. Teaching writing, like writing itself, is an unfolding and adaptable process.

To whatever extent possible I hope you will make room and time for your students to practice writing stories, whether they are fiction, nonfiction, or autobiography. I can offer all sorts of suggestions, but ultimately, commitment and patience on your part will generate the cumulative work that invites breakthroughs. People become stronger writers over time, with practice, and there is no way around that, no magic shortcut. If your students write consistently—and what better to write than stories?—and if you write, too, you will all develop and become stronger writers.

Which brings me to what may be, for some of you, the crux of the matter: your own writing. I am speaking directly to you—the writing teacher who writes, who wants to write, or who is tiptoeing toward writing scared to death. Everything in this book about writing is for you, too—every exercise, and bit of encouragement. I'll discuss approaches and exercises you might try with your students, but please know that I am saying them to you, too—about your own writing and your own creative process. Please, join with your students in taking the leap of faith that writing—and teaching—always are.

Part One

Entering into Stories

Chapter 1

ISSUING THE INVITATION
AND ASSORTED PRELIMINARIES

Rob Shepperson, my friend and collaborator on several books, drew this picture of me, and as soon as I saw it, I adopted it as my author portrait. I think it's a terrific picture of a writer—or, at least of me as writer.

First, I'm upside down. And I'm underwater. And my silent dog, Shadow, is there beside me. It says so many important things about my writing life. I am turned away from the usual way of thinking, standing, being. I am alone except for my black dog. And water: a whole other dimension. But I'm not drowning. It's mysterious. I must be breathing in a different way. I am in a different world.

How's that for an invitation to young writers: want to go to a different world? Just think how many kids are waiting to be asked, ready to jump at the chance.

Writing stories *is* their chance. Issue them the invitation. Invite yourself along for the ride, too.

Some will willingly accept. For others, the invitation to write will be off-putting or scary, tapping into preconceived notions of who they are and what they can and cannot do, yet another invitation for failure. For students who aren't particularly verbal or who are inclined to render their stories in other ways—or not to render them at all—the notion of committing words (not to mention thoughts and feelings) to paper is daunting. There will be some students whose spirits have already been smashed—heartbreaking as that reality is—and they will need special coaxing to come out and try again.

I like to tell them, all young writers, what riches await them.

First and foremost: power. So many children feel—and are—powerless most of the time. Writing is their personal chance to say something exactly as they see it, in their own voice. Having a strong, clear voice can make all the difference, and stories are a place to find that voice. I like to remind young writers: your stories give you a chance to set things straight, to show something exactly the way only you see it, to make things turn out exactly the way you want them to, the chance to control everything. And once a story has been written, it can be shared. Ultimately, (most) writers want to have their stories read. They write to communicate something they know, believe, or care about. Writing it in a story is one way to get the word out—many words, in fact—and a way to spread the word (their words) to whomever can and will read it.

Writing is also exquisitely democratic. Everyone with a story to tell has a chance at it, and everyone has a story to tell. Kids need to know that what they are thinking, imagining, and figuring out constitutes wonderful, rich, important material. No two people in the world have the same story to tell.

No matter how similar the topic, circumstances, or facts, every story is unique. I tell kids that they all hold secret stories inside them. Reminding students that no one else in the world could come up with the exact story they would write is just another way of reminding them that *they* are unique and precious: not a bad message—and an encouragement to get past the fear/worry that lurks in so many young writers (and writers of any age) that they have nothing new to say, that it's all been said before, and said better.

Something else to recommend writing stories: many of the best writers and most original voices I've ever encountered have not been the students with the best grades or most exemplary conduct records. That which can make for difficulties in classroom behavior can often make for good stories or at least a strong voice. Kids who have a definite take on the world have a leg up when it comes to writing stories, because they have something to say and they have conviction, which count for a lot in creating an interesting story that has some juice. Saying, "You could write about that" might, at times, become an alternative to a reprimand.

Some of the most resistant students, the angriest, wildest, most out-of-control, not to mention, the shyest and quietest kids, have written or told me lines or stories that will stay with me forever: brilliant, vibrant, thrilling expressions of themselves and the world around them. All bets are off when it comes to who's a great writer in-the-making. I love that. It might make a difference to your students, too—letting them know that when it comes to writing a good story the deck isn't stacked against any of them, in the classroom or in the world.

When my own children were growing up, I told them that, if they could learn to write a clear, perfect sentence that communicated exactly what they wanted, they'd be all set. So many "grown-up" jobs really come down to trying to communicate things clearly, so that other people can understand them. Being able to articulate a thought, fact, or feeling clearly in a human-sounding voice is a wonderful thing.

Another seductive call of writing, for me, anyway, is what an intensely private activity it can be. Writing is what taught me that I had thoughts, that I could think them whenever I wanted to, and that I could direct them. My thoughts were my own. They were free. They were always there for me to do something with, and they could go in a million different directions. All those realizations ushered me into my inner life, to a place I carried within, where I could always go, and where further exploration was always possible.

How Much We Already Have Going for Us

In a wonderful essay on the origins and life of narrative, Reynolds Price says,

> A *need to tell and hear stories is essential to the species* Homo sapiens—*second in necessity apparently after nourishment and before love and shelter. Millions survive without love or home, almost none in silence; the opposite of silence leads quickly to narrative, and the sound of story is the dominant sound of our lives.* (1985, 3)

Yes! We hunger for, feed on, and learn from stories from the time we're babies until the time we die. Sometimes I like to remind myself and my students that we don't need to turn it all into such a big deal. We can all get instantly scared or intimidated or lose our natural voices when we try to write a story. But stories sit inside us natural as breath. We tell our friends about what we did the night before, about the funny thing someone told us, about the weird guy we saw at the store, or about a dream we had. These are all stories. We choose what we want to tell from the millions of things that make an impression on us, large and small, instinctively picking material that has interested, amused, angered, confused, or amazed us. We make those choices, perform that act of discrimination, without much conscious thought. Our minds and hearts choose for us, quickly and without second guessing or premature editing. We jump in and start to tell the story (a beginning) and sooner or later (the middle) get to the point (the climax) and then wrap it up, often with some comment about what we made of it (the ending). We do this all the time, day in and day out—when we aren't listening to or watching the stories other people are telling us. Getting someone to tell you a story is usually not difficult either. Often it is just a matter of genuinely asking and listening attentively. We live in a world of stories, and we speak, sing, write, dream, and remember them quite naturally. We do it all the time.

Obviously, it's a huge leap from easily relating an anecdote to writing a well-crafted story, but we all harbor many of the ingredients of stories within us, along with storytelling muscles that we've been exercising most of our lives. Everyone can take heart from that and maybe relax a bit about the whole process. One more big and true thing: as writers, we are all in the same boat, up against and blessed by the same elements.

Daydreaming and Thinking About Thinking

When I was a little girl, riding my bike by myself around the neighborhood of our suburban development, I more than once pedaled straight into the back of a parked car. I still have a visceral memory of the utter shock of impact, of being catapulted—so rudely—out of my daydreams, off my bike, and into the street, only to be instantly overwhelmed with dread that someone might have witnessed my embarrassing freefall. What was I doing? Just daydreaming, so far inside my own thoughts, stories, and imagination that I couldn't see straight, couldn't see what was right in front of me—a parked car!

I sometimes tell students that daydreaming is probably the most important exercise of my writing life (and that sleep dreaming is also important) and that what I used to get in trouble for as a child, or fall off my bike because of, I now, as a published writer, get credit for.

Encouraging daydreaming may not sound like such a hot idea. Teaching's hard enough. However, giving young writers permission for extended imagining honors the fact that stories percolate in their own way, in their own sweet time.

If daydreaming is allowed and valued, you can occasionally slip in and ask, "What were you thinking?" and become privy to a most amazing answer, a privileged entry into a slit of a student's inner world. Seize that moment to praise someone's most private, interior thought as interesting, funny, imaginative, or the stuff of a good story, something to remember to put down on paper.

Many prompts and exercises demand a constantly moving pencil, never stopping, forcing words to come even if they feel meaningless or without conscious intent, and these exercises can uncork material for some people. But so can writing nothing, and simply daydreaming: going off by yourself into yourself, your imagination, and checking out what's there.

Supporting daydreaming in any way you can is an exercise in trust and hope. Ultimately, yes, a writer has to write; there's no way around that, but daydreaming has its place.

Some students will be intrigued by thinking about their thinking and watching what goes on inside their minds: tracking the things they wonder about, the stories or fantasies they make up, the flights of fancy, the imagined dialogues they engage in, the emotional roller coaster they ride.

Let your writers know that they have more going on inside of them than they might have realized. Interior thoughts, dreams, and fantasies can be a real eye-opener, like discovering a whole other apartment in a house you thought you knew well. Whatever age your students are, find the words and a way to talk to them about the unconscious. Invite them to access the thoughts, memories, images, day and night dreams simmering inside all of them. Again, it's beautifully democratic: everyone has an unconscious and interior thoughts to draw from, to nourish, and to get to know.

Discipline

Don't worry. Not all my preliminary musings about writing stories have to do with daydreaming and riding into parked cars. More than anything I consider writing to be an act of serious discipline.

When I was a kid, discipline had one meaning, and it involved nuns and meant that I was in trouble. It was not a desired outcome. Many years later, when I had the privilege of interviewing a group of Trappist monks, I was given a different take on the word—and the practice of—*discipline*, one that resonates deeply with my writing life.

With the monks, I witnessed a way of life that was highly ordered. Each day is divided into set times for praying, reading, contemplation, manual labor, eating, sleeping. The schedule is set in service to a life of worship, and there is an unmistakable simplicity, beauty, and order to it. One monk told me that leading a disciplined life made room for things to take hold and bloom.

What does this have to do with writing? The discipline of writing involves commitment and effort, some measure of silence and solitude, a schedule and setting conducive to productivity. Honoring the work of writing through established schedule and setting, approaching it with seriousness in an ordered way that works for the writer and is pleasing, these are all things that ultimately serve the story.

I've learned that cultivating a discipline helps me and benefits whatever piece of writing I am working on. Practicing discipline also makes me feel strong, like exercising. No, not *like* exercising. *Exercising*, the real thing—working hard and regularly. Taking my work seriously, honoring it with a set place and a committed schedule, giving it my deepest attention, all these things surround and support my writing.

We can cultivate habits and manners regarding how the work is handled, and we can work at being disciplined ourselves. We can all practice together.

Introducing students to discipline, to the notion of becoming a hard-working writer or person, is a gift we can give them. It's a wonderful and serious compliment to bestow upon someone: *you are a disciplined writer,* or *you are learning discipline.* Of course, a corresponding question then arises: how can we as teachers model discipline in our teaching, in the time and space we devote to writing, the attention we pay it, and the room we create for it? Serious invitations usually include a place and a time.

SCHEDULE: FINDING, MAKING, CARVING OUT TIME

It's a moment of reckoning for any serious writer, and for teachers of writing as well: what blocks of time will you commit to writing? Scheduling is challenging, and every writer and teacher I know struggles with it to some extent. In my classes with adults, I start by asking them to be realistic: how much time *can* they give/find/carve out for their writing given the realities of other work, family, and commitments? The same question applies here and now: how much time can you, a teacher, commit to writing in your classroom, with your students, given the demands of your specific school and schedule? It's better to assess honestly what time you can give and stick to it—honor it—than to make promises you can't keep. Every classroom, school, and school system is different, and all teachers answer to a host of demands. Do what you can, even if it seems like it's not enough. Some time is better than no time. Pale ink is better than a memory. (That bit of wisdom came to me years ago via a fortune cookie, and I've never forgotten it.)

What I've found over the years is that if you want to write, you *can* find the time. First, you need to believe that practicing writing stories will help your students (and you) become stronger writers. Once you begin and stick with it, you will see that for yourself.

I committed two hours twice a week to working on what became my first novel, *Tell Me Everything* (1993), while a babysitter watched my young son. For the most part, I wrote my second novel, *What Jamie Saw* (1995), in fifteen- to thirty-minute entries in my journal, before my children woke up in the morning and after a full day of work at another job, shortly before—or as—I fell asleep at night. These days I have the luxury of what was once unimaginable time to write. My time frames for teaching have varied widely, too. For years, I taught semester-long fiction workshops, meeting once a week for sixteen to twenty classes. During my years teaching in master of fine arts low-residency programs, I received five monthly packets of work from students over a six-month semester. I've taught day and weekend courses, visited many a classroom for just an hour or two. These days I teach an intensive weeklong Whole Novel Workshop twice a year. I try to make the most of any given arrangement, for either writing or teaching, and be reasonable about how far or deep I can go. The constraints of any given time period are a reality we all face. Honestly assess your own situation, and because you believe your students' writing is important, make as much time for it as you possibly can. Let the importance you place on writing and the respect you pay it become evident to your students.

SETTING

I can trace the path of my writing life over the years by thinking of the places where I've written: the corner desk in my childhood bedroom, my assigned desk in the study hall of my school, a library table in my first apartment, a converted bedroom, a converted closet, a borrowed room on the third floor of a friend's house, a converted barn, a lovely little cabin built on the foundation of an old chicken coop. No matter the location, the bottom-line truth remains the same: declaring and making a place of your own in which to write is an important act that bespeaks intention and seriousness. It honors the act and practice of writing. How can you and your students make the space you have in which to write special and inviting in its own way?

Given that most classrooms must serve and accommodate many different activities, you may not be able to dedicate much of the space solely to writing. But you can encourage your students to make places for themselves at home, in whatever nook or cranny they might find, in which to do their writing. You can invite their ideas for creating a writing space and a certain order or ritual around writing time. I have been in classrooms where such an order exists (very much tailored to each particular group of students), and it illuminates the young writers and the feel of their classrooms. You can also emphasize the things—the objects—connected to writing: computers, paper, pencils, notebooks, and pictures.

When I was in elementary school, we were required to write with fountain pens and thus had to carry around bottles of ink. I carried mine in a plastic container padded with rolled up tissue. That bottle of ink nestled in among the wad of tissue is one of the strongest, most pleasant memories I have from my school years. Do your students have some version of that special object or place that impresses upon them the importance, the specialness of what they are doing when they sit down to write? There are no correct answers to these questions except the answers you and your students come up with. You have to work within a set of parameters and conditions that are yours alone. You live in the real world, teach at a specific school, have more or less time and space to devote to writing in your classroom. Do what makes sense, do what you can, do what pleases you and your kids and encourages you all to write.

The Words We Use to Talk About Writing

I was introduced to the world of writing workshop in the classroom many years ago as a parent volunteer. I was also a working writer. As I came to know and practice the routine—the mini-lessons, the one-on-one conferences, the read-alouds—and as I became conversant with such vocabulary as *journaling* (a verb that still makes me shudder) and *sharing* and *author's chair*, I sometimes experienced an odd moment of disconnect as I thought, "Oh, this is like what I do!" Not *what* I do, but *like* what I do, because all the scaffolding around the writing—the terms, the prescribed steps to follow, the set notion of process—seemed a thing unto itself, one that sometimes eclipsed what it was set up to serve: writing. Words, phrases, and rules made the process of writing a story sound a lot more exact and straightforward than my experience of it ever was (or is, to this day).

The vocabulary of teaching writing came after-the-fact for me, a bunch of exact-sounding names for things that I usually thought of in terms of *muddling*, or *floundering*, or *adding stuff* or *cutting junk*, or *getting to the heart of the matter*.

Whatever helps a writer write a good, well-written story is what I care about. I don't need to tell you that each student learns in his or her own way. Of course, we'd all like the perfect explanatory statement, the technique or strategy that speaks to all. That, of course, does not exist. Young writers hear what they can hear at different times and in different ways. To that extent, we must try endless variations on getting our points across. Sometimes it's a matter of saying the same thing over and over until you happen to say it at just the moment that a young writer is ready to receive it. Other times it's a matter of saying it (whatever it is—*show don't tell; use specific details; have things happen in an order that makes sense; make sure your characters' voices sound real*) a million different ways, until you finally happen upon the way that this particular writer/child can understand.

Whatever words you use to describe the writing process and aspects of story are fine, as long as they help a writer write his or her story. That said, I am also aware of the demands many teachers face regarding state or national standards, the teaching of certain terms and definitions for various grade levels. Teach the terms, concepts, and definitions that are required; introduce the designated vocabulary. It's helpful to have terms that people can use in common to discuss and think about writing and the writing process. My plea is that you make the connection between those theoretical terms and concepts and the stories your students are writing and reading, in a way that makes real sense to them, perhaps using their own words to supplement the given definition.

THINKING UP YOUR OWN EXERCISES

I see writing exercises as attempts to solve problems, address struggles, move things forward: that's all. I devised exercises because I was stuck and needed help. I tried to think of ways to isolate a particular part of storytelling or writing technique that needed attention. There are tons of writing exercises and prompts in the vast literature that has risen up about how to write. Use the ones that work for you and your students. Steal from other people. Adapt exercises to better fit your group of writers. But don't think that you can't come up with some of your own. You never know what is going to be the approach that makes someone else understand something. And we all need to keep generating ideas because not every exercise works for every writer, and some writers aren't helped by exercises at all. Freewrites are torture for some writers. Maybe it's a little like food—it's OK to ask kids to try a bite, but I don't think we can make all writers eat all the same food all the time. Anything is all right as long as it serves the story and serves the writer who is trying to write it.

Some simple exercises that might accompany the invitation to write:

●◆ If you want to show your students that every person's story is different from everyone else's, offer a simple story line prompt—*Eli got a dog for a birthday present, but there was one little problem . . . A spaceship appeared on Tuesday night and made first contact by . . . Maria was sad to discover when she woke up that . . .* Dream up your own simple line or prompt, one that speaks to who your students are and where their interests lie. Let them write for a specified time, or have each of them simply write the next thing that happens or the next sentence—you can make this exercise as simple and quick or as long and involved as you like—and then have volunteers read their responses aloud. The story will instantly take different twists and turns. You can point out the wide range of plot developments, tones, settings, details, and word choices. Given the same starting point and the same information, everyone makes something of it that is all their own. Gradually, your students will start to trust that they might have something unique to say, part of who they alone are. Now, you can say, what if you told a story you cared deeply about, one that came from inside you?

➤ Some young writers may be interested in keeping a dream journal, filled with the stuff of day and night dreams: words, images, or both.

➤ Or here's a simple exercise that might help your students become more aware of their minds and their thinking: simply have them sit in silence for one, two, or three minutes with their eyes closed. At the end of the minutes of silence, have them write down (or draw or make symbols for) as many things as they can remember—ideas, thoughts, memories, sensations, images—that passed through their mind. The list will undoubtedly be a hodge-podge, a bombardment, from just several moments. Realizing that there is so much ongoing chatter in our minds can be an eye-opener, as can the notion that we can watch ourselves thinking. What does this have to do with writing? It speaks to paying attention to what is going on inside, to identifying thoughts and choosing the most interesting and intriguing ones to follow. All these things play a part in writing. In any case, this exercise gives everyone a few moments of silence, and that's never bad.

➤ As for terms and definitions: Keep a running list of terms and definitions you and your young writers come up with for plot, theme, structure—all the parts of a story—and the stages of writing one. List them along with the "official" definitions you and they are required to master. Your young writers will come up with brilliant descriptors that speak to them in their own voices about a process that is messy, crooked, and different for everyone. (For inspiration, check out Ruth Krauss and Maurice Sendak's wonderful book *A Hole Is to Dig* [1952].) The ways we talk about writing and process need not be words spoken from on high.

- Invite your students to tell stories aloud. Give them a short and set time limit—the thirty-second story, the one-minute story, the three-minute story. Settle on a chosen topic—close calls, scariest moments, biggest surprises—and then choose a few volunteers. Your storytellers will become accustomed to getting to the point sooner than later, editing out all but the important and essential information. Ask those who have listened to the story to name the part that sticks with them the most. You will hear some amazing stories, some wonderful expressions, some revealing insights, and you can point out and praise all those things, making the link to using them in the written version of the story. At all times, in any encounter, practice listening for and praising the anecdotes, expressions, or word choice a student may use in speaking with you.

- Finally, once you and your students have been writing for a while, I wonder what each of *your* author portraits might look like? Are you upside down, underwater, too? Up in the sky, perhaps? Do you have chains? (I hope not.) Wings, maybe? I wonder.

Chapter 2

Finding and Molding Material

Flannery O'Connor's famous statement that "anybody who has survived his childhood has enough information about life to last him the rest of his days" (1969, 84) has special resonance when you think about young people writing. They are in the midst of such a truly fertile time of their lives. How are they to realize that? It's simply what *is* for them. As teachers, we may not be able to convince our young writers that their day-to-day experiences constitute rich material—that which adult authors endlessly mine and return to as the seeds of everything—but we can encourage them to value what is theirs and what is all around them: the voices they hear, with whatever accents, lilt, or particular expressions; the objects, the things they play with and love and trade and lose; the particularity of the life they lead, where they lead it, and how they spend their hours and days. Young writers can draw from wonderful raw material, a sea of emotional, physical, and intellectual challenges and upheavals. They know plenty, and stories can be their chance to show what they know, hope, or wonder about. They all live in families of one sort or another. What do they know from that, and what do they know from their interactions with their friends or their lack of friends? They *do* know something, and a story is where they can make what they know perfectly clear, whether they choose to address issues through unfiltered autobiography or by creating a fictional cast of characters and events where they are free to determine the outcome. One life is not "better" than another when it comes to writing; everything is fair game. Material is universal and all around us. Good stories grow out of what we make of that material, what we choose to gather, and how we shape and render it.

When I dreamed of being a writer more than I actually wrote, I lamented that I had grown up more or less in suburbia, feared that I had not suffered enough, that the kind of madness in my family didn't hold a candle to the madness in Jane Eyre's. I dismissed almost out of hand the dramatic worth or potential of my own life, simply because it was, well, familiar. I already had a notion that great writers needed to write about Big Important Things, which were, of course, beyond me and, of which, of course, I knew nothing. Then I started reading more. I remember reading my first Jane Austen novel and thinking, amazed, it's really OK to write about these things? Flirtation, gossip, descriptions of the tiniest and most revealing habit? Then I read Virginia Woolf, and I couldn't *believe* where *she* had gone, how far in she got. Bit by bit it began to dawn on me that *everything* was possible material. Reading showed me that I could journey inwardly into heart and soul as much as outwardly into the world, and that small moments held worlds within them and treasures of their own. If we can let kids know that they already have within them all the ingredients for storytelling and encourage them to value themselves, their lives, and their imaginations, perhaps they can bypass the detour of believing they have nothing to write about and no stories worth telling.

WHERE DO YOU GET YOUR IDEAS?

Readers of all ages ask the question, "Where do your stories come from?" as if there might be a special repository where real writers know the good stash of ideas is hidden. The truth is we live in the stash, and we harbor the stash within us. I tell kids that they have stories in them if they have questions, if they have memories, if they have strong feelings, if they wonder about why things are the way they are, if they have a past, live in the present, have hope for the future.

My ideas come from everywhere, from all around and inside me, from everything capable of making an impression on me, especially those things that make a lasting, searing impression. For instance, here's where the idea for the opening of *What Jamie Saw* (1995) came from. Many years ago—and years before I started writing *What Jamie Saw*—my dear friend Peggy Laufer (who is one of the teachers to whom this book is dedicated) told me this family story: Her great aunt was pushing her baby in a baby carriage to meet up with a group of other mothers and their babies at a park in New Jersey. The park was a triangular plot of land surrounded by busy, trafficked streets. After crossing the road into the park, Peggy's aunt saw a car careening out of control, headed straight toward her and the other mothers and babies. She had just a moment to think what to do: the out-of-control car was barreling toward them. In a split instant, Peggy's aunt reached into the baby carriage, grabbed her baby, and threw him, over to the side, away from where they all were standing!

The car hit. One person was killed and others were hurt, including Peggy's aunt Bea. Her baby, Donald, who had landed safely in a pile of leaves off to the side, was unharmed.

When Peggy told me that story, I gasped when she said that her aunt threw the baby! I had an immediate mental image of a tiny baby sailing through the air. Clearly that image made a lasting and deep impression on me, because years later, when I was struggling to write a story about a little boy named Jamie who I knew was scared of something—that image of the thrown, flying baby came back to me, as fresh and clear as the night Peggy told me the story. I took it (like the good thief every writer is) and molded it to fit the story I wanted to write, and this is what it became:

When Jamie saw him throw the baby, saw Van throw the baby, saw Van throw his little sister Nin, when Jamie saw Van throw his baby sister Nin, then they moved.

. . . It wasn't the crying that woke him up. It was some other sound—what was it?—something else that made him spring up in bed, eyes wide, just in time to see Van reach into the crib and grab Nin and throw her, fire her across the room, like a missile, like a bullet, like a shooting star, like a football. No: like nothing Jamie'd ever seen before.

And quicker than Jamie could even take in what he's just seen, quicker than any beginning or middle could possibly be, he saw the ending: saw his mother catch her, catch his baby sister Nin—there, plop, in her arms. Saw his mother step out of the dark hallway and into the lighted bedroom and raise up her arms, as if she'd been waiting her whole life to appear at that moment, exactly in that place, to raise up her arms and catch her flying baby.

So, you see, the flying baby is still there, front and center, still a cause for gasping, but very different from the baby in the story Peggy told me. In my version, the mother saves the flying baby by catching her, and in the real story, the flying baby was saved by being thrown. These are observations I see now, after the fact. At the time that I wrote the opening of *What Jamie Saw*, I wasn't thinking about anything but the image of the flying baby. I don't know that I was thinking anything at all, consciously. I was using something—an image that had produced an almost electric shock response in me—to get my story going.

That's one example of one seed of a story—a seed that was planted in me through another story and stored away until the time was right for harvesting. Now, whenever I hear, see, or am told something that takes my breath away, that shocks me with its force, I pay attention. I make note of it. I respect its power. Such moments, images, and exchanges may find their way into stories, hugely altered but still carrying an emotional punch. All of us are exposed to all sorts of ideas, images, and situations that are the stuff of stories. The trick is to be on the lookout for them, to store them away, and to practice summoning them when needed.

I often tell students that they need elephant ears to listen for the ideas that will start their stories, the voices that will speak inside them, and the sounds that will bring them to life.

Writers must be good listeners to render voices that sound real and natural. They need to be good watchers, too; they need Big Eyes for seeing everything around them—what all the places and people look like, down to the tiniest gesture and detail. Watching and listening are not passive acts: they are essential and serious work for writers.

When it comes to getting a story started, I'm a big believer in following crumbs. Start with whatever comes to you—a memory, a big question, a detail or gesture, a bit of dialogue, a certain place. In my experience, stories don't arrive whole and realized, needing only to be put down on paper. For me, they come in layers or steps, one thing at a time, building up. So whenever you get one thing—even a crumb—take it, say thank you, and go from there. Ideas, phrases, words, details, and images that come unbidden are of special interest to me—organic material to consider. They may not be the things that end up in the final story, but they often are the crumbs that jump-start it.

I loved learning that The Chronicles of Narnia by C. S. Lewis— *The Lion, The Witch and The Wardrobe* (2000), among them—grew out of an image that appeared unbidden in the writer's mind one day: a faun standing by an old-fashioned lamppost in the snow. That image *did* remain in the final story—and what a lovely and magical image it is—and is a perfect example of a single out-of-the-blue gift that a writer knew enough to pursue.

A story contains many elements—character, action, setting, theme, and voices—and an idea for a story can come from or speak to any one of those elements. As teachers, we need to train our young writers to recognize and be on the lookout for a good story kernel.

Links Between Autobiography and Fiction

Young readers often ask me whether the stories I've written really happened. They want to know whether the things that my main characters go through are things I experienced when I was young. They hunger to know what is real, what is true, and the level of separation between the story and real life, between author and character. These are wonderful concepts for you to discuss with your writers and for them to examine as they write their own stories. Such discussions will naturally lead into considering different genres, such as fiction, nonfiction, memoir, and personal narrative. One genre is not better than another, and the borders between them are often unclear; stories can be hybrids. Good story writing techniques will serve them all.

It's quite likely your students will write stories in which they are, consciously or unconsciously, the main character. Some writers are comfortable writing autobiographical stories or personal narratives, and some writers instinctively veer off toward fiction/fantasy, playing fast and loose with what happens in the story but still keeping themselves (or a version of themselves) at the center of the action.

Autobiography is a wonderful genre, and autobiographical material is a reliable jumping-off point for writing fiction. Many young writers, at least those who are not instantly committed to fantasy and science fiction, start off writing stories that are very close to "what really happened." That choice can also prove inhibiting. At some point, many young writers who consciously draw on heavily autobiographical material worry about exposing themselves and the other people they write about. This is a valid concern that deserves consideration and discussion (and one that goes hand in hand with concerns you may need to address in your classroom regarding appropriate and acceptable topics). Writing stories is not about getting back at people or violating anyone's privacy.

Writing fiction offers the writer a chance to change and mold autobiographical material—from assigning different names to characters, to altering some of what happened, to coming up with a completely different outcome—and thereby allows them degrees of separation from the incident or character that may have inspired the story. Those acts of alteration, whether small or large, often are the first steps writers take in the journey into fiction. They tiptoe away from autobiography and deeper into fiction as they become conscious of their need and power to do so, and as they acquire the tools for doing so. It can be a mind-expanding realization for young writers to discover that characters exist separate from the writer, even if the story is completely autobiographical.

For me, the key to moving deeper and deeper into fiction was learning that I could apply familiar feelings, emotional responses, and interior states to situations and circumstances beyond my own limited experience. Trusting the universality of feelings, such as loss, grief, fear, hope, and love, allowed me to venture into story lines that hadn't "really happened" to me. I didn't have to lose my mother as a child (as my protagonist Roz did in *Tell Me Everything* [1993]) to write authentically about the grieving process. I didn't have to suffer domestic violence (as Jamie and his mother did in *What Jamie Saw* [1995]) to write authentically about trauma and fear. I had experienced versions of them in my own life, and I drew on my heart's memory. The old adage "write what you know" has more to do with what you know in your heart, than situations and circumstances you may have personally experienced. Research can go a long way in providing necessary facts and history. For something to ring true on the page, it needs to be emotionally true, to have an interior authority.

We all reveal ourselves in our writing, which is one reason that writing can be such a scary proposition. The stories our young writers write, regardless of whether they're conscious of it, reveal questions, concerns, fears, and dreams they harbor.

When I first started writing short stories, they were often prompted by something that made me angry, something that struck me as off or unfair, something I wanted to bring to light. In writing the story, however, the anger invariably gave way to something else, moved beyond where it had started from in a way I would never have known had I not made a story out of it. Writing the story transformed what had started it, and the transformation shaped the story. It was my first inkling that the stories take on a life of their own (as do characters, no matter how closely drawn from real-life people) and have certain demands that must be answered. "Serve the story" became a guiding light for me. What does the *story* need to make it work—that's the real question, not what do I, the writer, need? Or what really happened? Or what's the rule to follow? What does the story *itself* need to work, to get to where it needs to go?

Fiction is, largely, about change, and writing fiction changes things. It doesn't take long before a writer (of any age) comes to see that that a story, once it starts to become a real story, has its own trajectory, characters, and needs, and it must be served and tended to. It may start out being one way, with a certain intention or instigating event, but it becomes, in the writing of it, its own animal. I have come to rely on and trust in this process of transformation, a saving grace for me and my stories.

WHAT'S APPROPRIATE?

Some of my earlier books in particular deal with dark subject matter—domestic violence, grief, incest. A number of reviewers and adult readers I spoke with questioned whether such subject matter was appropriate for children (of any age). Some books and topics will always generate controversy. Librarians and teachers are sometimes called on to navigate rocky terrain in answering those who might question the appropriateness of a certain book, discussion, or in-class writing assignment. I acknowledge and wholeheartedly sympathize with the myriad of considerations teachers must take into account. There are no simple answers and many points of view. Here is my opinion regarding tackling difficult material and the use of tough language.

"How come you used swears?" I heard that question, or a variation of it, many times when I visited classrooms after writing *What Jamie Saw*. The kids got a little excited even asking it, as if tiptoeing into dangerous territory. As a writer, I find dangerous territory irresistible, but that has nothing to do with why some of my characters sometimes swear. I explained that my characters really talked that way, and that dialogue is the sound of real-sounding voices. I also told them that my editor and publisher also agreed that those words were necessary for that story; many people are involved in making a book, and many people have a say in what works and what doesn't. My real answer to the students came in the form of more questions for them: "Did those words shock you? Scare you? Have you never heard those words before?" Everyone laughed at the last question. "So, if you have heard words like that plenty of times before, why is it a big deal to see them in a book? Do you think that because some of my characters talk like that I, as a writer, am recommending that *you, or anyone*, should talk like that? What would happen if you talked like that? The last question elicited enthusiastic response and stories. I contributed this one:

I overheard an argument between a high school boy and girl outside my window. The boy used profanity in every single sentence, sometimes in between words. He was angry, and the words he used to show it were the same few swear words inserted all over the place. The longer I listened, the more it struck me how much his words got in the way of his sounding smart or of his getting his point across. His swearing took up too much space and kind of gobbled up the words that came before and after and, in the end, robbed him of what he might have been trying to say. Only his emotion—anger—came across. So, in that case, I thought the swears were a little sad. Sometimes I think they can be funny, and sometimes they can really emphasize a point. However, swears never scare me. The use of a word, any word, is a choice. How do you want to come across? What do you mean to say?

That's the way I feel about words and not everyone agrees with me, but isn't it better to have a discussion about it—even if there are set rules that have to be followed—so that kids can have another opportunity to think about the uses of language? Considering the power of words seems to me a better way to go than simply laying down rules point-blank.

As for tough subject matter, what's appropriate and what's off-limits? Nothing is for me. What about for you? And why is that? What would you say is off-limits for your students, and why?

I don't know until I read something whether I feel it's off, sick, scary, or gratuitous. Anything can be all right. Anything can be all wrong. A lot depends on the intention. Why is the writer writing this? What is the writer after? Secrets are often the stuff of good stories, and secrets live in the dark before they are brought into the light.

Having said all this, all I really want to do is encourage you to know why you set the limits you do, and do your best to help your students understand, too.

CHOICE OF MATERIAL AND GENRE

Choice is something most people of any age appreciate having. Writers are constantly choosing, consciously or unconsciously, what to write about, how to write it, what to include, what to cut, and what words to use. Every step along the way, they need to make choices so that their story will be the one they mean to tell. As teachers, we need to make them more conscious of all the choices they have.

Often not *everything* is up to the writer. Sometimes we step in and assign topics or give particular prompts. We set guidelines and page limits and focus on autobiography, fiction, or nonfiction. When that's the case, it is important to be clear about what the goals and parameters of the story are.

EXERCISES FOR FINDING AND MOLDING MATERIAL

- *Drawing on Memories:* Certainly, all your students harbor memories that have made an impression on them. They can mine their memories for incidents, moments, exchanges, and images that, for whatever reason, have imprinted on their minds and in their hearts. No editing or judging is necessary. Remembering is an exercise that no one can do wrong—my favorite kind.

Teachers can help by listening to someone's memory of something and talking about what the writer finds most interesting. There is usually a point in the conversation when what interests the writer interests the listener, and that's often a good place for the writer to start putting words on paper. Of course, there are plenty of times that the writer is sitting on a gold mine of an interesting story that he or she doesn't recognize because it's "just my life" or "just what happened." We all tend to dismiss what is familiar to us, the given of our lives. Sometimes it takes a careful listener to point out that what someone else knows and takes for granted is interesting.

I had a high school student tell me in passing about her total immersion baptism at age fifteen in an Arkansas lake. She was stunned by my interest in hearing more about it. She had a perfectly clear and vivid memory of it, but she was unaware of its powerful impact on others until she received a listener's feedback. It's one of our jobs as teachers to be on the lookout for what a writer knows—holds in his or her memories or consciousness—that is amazing, interesting, or funny. Not just the obvious things, either. They're the easy ones to pick up on. We also have to be on the lookout (and the listen-up) for the subtler, nuanced thoughts, memories, and ideas that our writers harbor.

I hope that "You could write about that," or "How about writing about that?" become common phrases in your classroom, planting the notion all the time, as thoughts, ideas, and comments come up that reveal an attitude, a history, a certain take on things that has particular energy, voice, spark.

●◆ *A Tip-Toe into Fiction Exercise:* Ask your students to write about something that happened to them but to change the names of all the characters. They'll have fun choosing new names and might be surprised by how different the story sounds to them—the sense of distance it creates—to make that simple alteration.

Now ask them to create a completely different ending for the story. This can be their chance to make a sad story happy or a happy story sad. It's a quick way to show them the power that fiction offers. Remind them, however, that they have to make it credible. They'll need to think about a different ending that is sensible and plausible, given what has come before it.

●◆ *A Sampler of Questions for Finding Material and Maybe Starting a Story:* As I was writing my middle-grade romp, *Sneaking Suspicions* (2007), I made a list of basic considerations and central concerns of the story. After the book was published and I was asked to visit schools, I turned that list into a series of questions to share with students. They're the kind of basic questions that easily and naturally elicit stories. Here is that list:

> What's the most complicated thing you've ever
> tried to understand?
> What's something you have serious doubts about?

What's something you worried about that turned out to be really OK?

Did you ever suspect that someone was up to something no good?

Do you think the glass is half-empty or half-full?

If you could build your own town, what would you name it?

What would be one rule everyone in your town had to live by?

If you made a fortune, how much of it would you give away and to whom/for what?

Can you think of a good example of crooked thinking?

Who is the most generous person you know? What does the person give?

What does your family have that you think is worth the most?

What is something you have that you consider terribly valuable?

What foods are you afraid to eat and why?

What's a story that you know that has more than one version?

Which version do you like the best?

What's the most real thing in the world to you?

What's something you consider fake?

What's the most valuable thing you ever lost? Did you find it?

How would you design your family crest? What would the motto be?

What's the best present you ever gave someone?

Start your own list of juicy questions, in your own words. Keep it simple. You'll know you've got it right when there isn't anything the slightest bit intimidating about the questions, and responses to them come naturally, loaded with rich details.

Chapter 3

Peter Rabbit and the Shape of a Story

$\mathcal{B}$efore considering the component elements contained in story, I want to offer two overarching ways of looking at story that have helped me as both writer and teacher.

The first has to do with the narrative arc—a literary term that describes the shape of a story: its beginning, middle, and end; its rising action; and its climax and resolution. The narrative arc serves as a touchstone for me in both writing and responding to a story. It's a basic road map that helps me track and understand stories of all kinds.

From Aristotle on, many folks have expounded on the subject of narrative arc, but the clearest and simplest way I know to see it in action is to look at Beatrix Potter's *The Tale of Peter Rabbit* (1902). At least that's how I really *got* the notion of *complication* and *resolution*: the clarifying distinctions among beginning, middle, and end. Whatever your students' ages, this perfect little book has much to say and show about what a story is and what makes it work.

I was invited to consider the work of Beatrix Potter in *How to Read a Novel* (1957), an adult book by Caroline Gordon, an accomplished novelist and short-story writer of her time. In one chapter, she analyzes Sophocles' *Oedipus Rex* to show how it adheres to and fulfills Aristotle's rules regarding complication and resolution. But then she relates how, while reading *Jemima Puddle-Duck* to her grandchild, she discovered, "somewhat to my surprise," that "Miss Potter was not only a master of her own medium but a master of some of the same technical devices which Sophocles used to such admirable effect in *Oedipus Rex*" (Gordon 1957, 25).

Gordon turned me back to the work of Beatrix Potter with a new eye, at a time when I was struggling to learn how to write a good story and how to make it work from beginning to end. In their simplicity and clarity, Potter's books felt like they'd been sent from heaven to help me. I focused on one of her masterpieces, *The Tale of Peter Rabbit*. Identifying its narrative arc gave me a way to see the overall *shape* of a story, how its various parts worked together and added up to something greater than the sum of its parts.

See for yourself: open this book, so thoughtfully conceived and published to fit in a small hand, and right away, through picture and word, be invited into the unfolding drama. We, the readers, are introduced, without fuss or bother, to Peter Rabbit and his siblings and offered a clear and concise description of where they live. The reader is immediately grounded in a specific place, with named characters. Without further ado, the story moves forward, partly by introducing important information from the past: Mrs. Rabbit warns her children not to venture into Mr. McGregor's garden, lest they end up like their father—baked in a pie! The pictures are delicious and inviting, the tone is light and cautionary, and the stakes are life or death! Tension is introduced with the warning. Having set up the main threat (or possible problem), Mrs. Rabbit takes her leave, going to the store to buy "a loaf of brown bread and five currant buns." How perfectly specific the author is! The beginning of the story has done all it needs to do: introduce the main characters, introduce the problem or threat, and set the action in motion.

Once mother is off-stage, the plot immediately thickens. While his sisters do as they were told, Peter sneaks away and crawls into Mr. McGregor's garden. Because the reader has been clued into the past history regarding his father and the pie, the reader understands that Peter is in danger. Tension—a key element in any story—is quickly established. Potter has also distinguished the characters from one another by noting that Flopsy, Mopsy, and Cottontail were "good little bunnies" and that Peter was "very naughty." The reader has a sense of who the characters are, through the illustrations and the text, and how differently they behave.

What happens next? The focus is now entirely on Peter—it's his story, after all—and he eats and eats some more, and, then, because he ate so much, he goes looking for parsley. He is in a dangerous place, but so far he seems safe.

The turn of the page brings a major ratcheting up of the tension when he happens upon Mr. McGregor!

Things now move quickly. There's a lot of action in the middle of the story. Mr. McGregor chases Peter. Peter runs, loses his shoes, and gets his big brass buttons tangled in the net on the gooseberry bush. Lots of verbs! And you have to love the chosen details! And, then, for just a moment—a page spread—the story zooms in to reveal Peter's emotional state, his exhaustion at the point of nearly giving up, just before the birds appear to *implore him to exert himself.*" (How much Beatrix Potter must have loved choosing those exact words!)

Once again he is off and running. Peter makes a last-minute escape from Mr. McGregor and hides in a watering can. Mr. McGregor comes looking. Peter sneezes, and once again the tension is ratcheted higher and things don't look good for Peter! Then, in the nick of time, Peter makes it through the window and Mr. McGregor gives up his chase.

Pause. The tension is momentarily released. But this is not the end. There are still other problems to solve: Peter must find his way out of the garden. He is wet and cold from the watering can. There are possible solutions, but he is thwarted. He finds a door, but can't squeeze through; the mouse can't help him because her mouth is full. He sees a cat but knows enough to be wary of cats. The tension is controlled. New things keep happening. The reader wants to know how it will all turn out.

Finally, Peter catches sight of the wall, races to it, and is out and safe before Mr. McGregor can get to him. He is back outside the garden, where he started from. The main problem of the story has been solved; the reader is reassured. Now, all we need to know is the aftermath of it all. The consequences of what he did. And there *are* consequences, because this is a moral tale—that is, a story that has something to say about certain types of behavior—and they play out over the final pages of the story: Peter's clothes that he lost during his escape attempts are used by Mr. McGregor on a scarecrow. Peter gets a cold and has to go to bed and drink chamomile tea, while his sisters get to have bread, milk, and blackberries. The resolution is complete. With a limited number of words and an accompanying collection of exquisite paintings, a complete and satisfying story has been told—beginning, middle, and end.

Surely, I'd been taught or told about narrative arc prior to reading Gordon's analysis, but somehow draping *Peter Rabbit* over that arc finally allowed the concept to take root in me. Perhaps it happened because I was finally *ready* to have it take root: what Gordon was telling me mattered because I was trying to write my own stories, beginning to end. I never cared a bit about the narrative arc before that. None of the things I learned about literary devices, structure, or even punctuation ever mattered *all* that much to me until I wanted to write stories of my own. I learned rules of grammar and punctuation for the tests I had to take, and I learned about similes, exposition, and other such terms, as well. But they all began to matter in a deep and true way when I began working on my own stories. Then I hungered to understand how stories were built and what they were built with (words, sentences, paragraphs, scenes). Then the narrative arc became a simple and clear map, one that's always there for me in every story I write. It doesn't necessarily *have* to be followed, but it offers the tried and true shape of a journey, and that's what most stories come down to.

Using the narrative arc as a formula and applying arbitrary characters and events will not produce a satisfying story. The choice of material is crucial—the content must mean something to the author, and the things that happen in the story must make sense and connect to one another. Once rich material has been chosen, the narrative arc can be a reference tool, a gauge, something that offers an overview of the whole story. It can help a reader see inside to a story's structure and help a writer order his or her material. The simple and beautiful shape of the arc can remind all of us that a story needs to keep moving forward, building toward climax and resolution. Most of my guiding lights in writing a story are simple and basic, things I return to time and time again to help me get my bearings—and the narrative arc is one of them.

Carolyn Gordon's (1957) analysis of *Jemima Puddle-Duck* and *Oedipus Rex* happened to be my way into seeing the basic structure and shape of a story; maybe a deeper look into *Peter Rabbit* will help you and your students. Whether it's an eye-opener or not, considering this simple tale allows you to point out the basic structure of story to your students, to introduce the concepts of beginning, middle, and end—rising tension or complication, climax and resolution. Because of its necessarily limited amount of text and beautiful artwork, it's easy to point out exceptionally good word choice and detail. Best of all, considering this picture book together with your students allows you to start asking the basic questions that will come up again and again as your students start to write stories of their own:

Whose story is it? Who does the story belong to?
What are the most important events that happen in the story and in what order do they happen?
What's the main character's dominant character trait?
How does the main character respond to what happens?
What's the turning point in the story?
Does the main character change as a result of what happens?
What is this story about?
How does this story make you feel?

Whether you explore the narrative arc with your students prior to their working on their own story writing is up to you and depends, to some extent, on their capacity to entertain abstract concepts. Once they are involved in writing their own stories, referring to the lessons of *Peter Rabbit* will take on greater resonance. As a teacher, having a solid understanding of story structure and shape will offer you a platform from which to respond to all the stories that come your way. (I have more to say about how you can respond to the structure of a story in Chapter 13.)

Exercises to Help Introduce the Concept of Narrative Arc

- ➡ Help your students get a feel for the narrative arc and the shape of a story within themselves. Choose a song that's currently popular among them, or a tune that is familiar to all—a Christmas carol, "Twinkle Twinkle Little Star," "Happy Birthday." Have your students sing the song right up until the last word and then stop. Everyone will experience the almost physical call for completion and resolution. It will produce a funny feeling of denied expectation or fulfillment that you can liken to the call for a satisfying ending to stories. Or have them sing a certain line of the song over and over until the repetition makes your students squirm: you'll be showing them the need to keep a story moving forward toward resolution.

- ➡ Look into a story that the entire class has read in terms of the narrative arc. Ask your students to iden-tify the beginning of the story, the scenes that build the tension and move the story forward, the climax and the resolution. The more they internalize this basic structure, the better chance they have of shaping their own stories in a clear and satisfying way.

    I use *Peter Rabbit* as a way of showing narrative arc and other essential elements of a story. It is also, of course, an exquisitely rendered picture book, a classic of that exacting and wonderful form. People who think that creating a picture book is easy or simple to pull off are naive. It's as easy to do as it is to write a perfect poem and draw like an angel. That said, it can be a wonderful challenge to give to students of all ages: to create a picture book of their own, working separately or in creative teams of author/artist. This is a serious undertaking and a demanding form. It needs to be given time and attention. If you decide to try it, I recommend that you do research in advance, including Uri Shulevitz's *Writing with Pictures* (1985) and Selma G. Lanes's *The Art of Maurice Sendak* (1993). In creating a picture book, your students will answer to the necessity of telling a complete story in limited text spread over (no more than) 32 pages, a form of discipline all its own that will only help them when it comes to writing short stories. They will exercise muscles of choosing, paring down their text, discriminating between what is revealed through pictures and what is revealed through text, and considering beginning, middle, and end.

Chapter 4

PLOT OF ACTION
AND PLOT OF CHARACTER

The distinction between character-driven stories and plot-driven stories is another overarching way of looking at story that has helped and guided me in my writing. It's a big and basic distinction and offers an understanding that can be a touchstone for both writer and teacher.

As simple as it is, I was slow to really get it. My editor had to articulate it over and over as I struggled to write my first plot-driven book (*The Big House* [2004]) after working for years on finely nuanced, character-driven stories (*What Jamie Saw* [1995], *Tell Me Everything* [1993], *Bee and Jacky* [1998], *Many Stones* [2000]). Each type of story emphasizes different elements and calls on the writer to exercise different muscles.

Some stories are most concerned with what happens: the action, the events, the pure adventure. These stories are plots of action. *Treasure Island* (1985), by Robert Louis Stevenson, for instance, is a classic example. These stories call for clear and exciting episodes arranged in a sequence that builds tension and moves the story along at a relatively fast pace, leading to a grand and satisfying climax. Main concerns for action-based stories include crafting carefully chosen plot developments and pacing and sequencing them for the greatest effect.

In plots of action, all scenes/episodes are essentially *transitional*: they get the hero from this situation to the next situation and then to the next. First, the hero fights the guard at the bridge. Then the hero is captured on the other side of the bridge by the squad who take him to jail. Then the hero overcomes the guards at the jail and escapes out the window. Then the hero confronts the monsters in the inner courtyard of the castle that protect the bad guy who has the princess prisoner. Then the hero kills the monsters and breaks into the keep. Then the bad guy threatens to kill the princess and so forth. Each episode is basically the same: the hero encounters an obstacle or opponent that he either vanquishes or is vanquished by. You can shuffle the episodes although the blocking forces tend to increase in strength.

The characters certainly have a role to play in these stories, but the story is not (mainly) about their personal growth; they may or may not change as a result of what happens. The protagonist of an action-based story is often a hero, who, over the course of events, owns who he or she always was in the first place or who leaves home on a journey or quest and is finally able to return home. A plot of action is a compelling sequence of events that affect the main character for better or for worse. The reader usually hopes that when all is said and done, the character is better off (e.g., lives happily ever after) than he or she was at the beginning. A plot of action is primarily about what happens and how it happens.

A character-driven story, however, *is* most concerned with character—who the character is and how he or she changes over the course of the narrative. *Little Women* (1994) by Louisa May Alcott is a good example. The character's emotional journey propels the narrative forward. The writer takes the time and space to explore his or her heart and mind. The key questions writers ask in creating character-driven stories are, What does my character want? What is my character's heart's desire? What is my character dying for lack of? How does my character change? What is my character up against? What is my character's emotional journey? (There are wonderful and endless variations on these questions. You and your students will come up with some of your own, no doubt.) In a character-driven story, the writer must know all along the way what is inside his or her character's heart and mind and how that character evolves.

In a plot of character, scenes are essentially *incremental*: they reveal the protagonist's development of consciousness. In Jane Austen's *Pride and Prejudice* (2009), for example, at first Elizabeth Bennet considers Darcy a snob. Then she witnesses his refined taste and generosity and wonders whether she might be mistaken. In their next encounter, Elizabeth is not so judgmental, and then she believes he has acted badly and once again dislikes him. Finally, she understands his behavior and allows her affection for him to blossom. Elizabeth changes bit by bit. Her emotional response to Darcy swings back and forth, eventually moving to the next level of openness. Scenes reveal the gradual evolution of her character that enables the development of her love for Darcy to take place. Darcy's character doesn't change; Elizabeth's perception of him, and herself, does. Because of the nature of the incremental changes, the order of the episodes in character-based stories is critical.

Of course, in *all* stories, character and plot intersect. Characters act and are affected by things that happen, and things that happen have to happen to someone. Action-based stories have wonderful characters, and character-driven stories have delicious plot lines. Probably the most satisfying stories perfectly merge compelling plots and irresistible characters. However, most stories usually emphasize one over the other, and they all take their place somewhere on the continuum. In my own stories and in those I critique, I always find it helpful to understand what the balance is, or wants to be, so I can consciously address just how to strike that balance.

In my experience with younger writers, many boys gravitate toward action-driven stories; girls are often inclined toward character-driven stories. Most writers I've worked with (of all ages and either gender) are naturally inclined toward one kind of story over the other. One is not better than the other; they're just different. They speak to different appetites.

Once, years ago, when I'd hit the wall with my novel-in-progress, I turned for help to my son, David, a big fan of action-based stories. I told him what I knew about the story up to that point, describing the characters and what they were up against. I ran through a bunch of options I was considering to ratchet up the tension and to keep the novel moving. He listened without responding as I suggested one lame plot development after another. Finally, when I was done, he shrugged and said, "Turn them all into vampires."

That was *years* before *Twilight*! If only I had listened! But the fact is that I didn't. Couldn't. Wouldn't. His instinctive response has stayed with me, though, and speaks directly to our different appetites for different kinds of stories.

Invite your writers to think about what interests them most: what makes people tick or what happens? As writers, do they want to delve into a person's heart and mind and track how he or she grows, changes, comes to a new place? Do they wonder why people behave the way they do? Are they captivated by the dynamics of relationship, by how people treat one another? Or are they more drawn to surprising events and developments, twists and turns of plot, exciting action?

Some will land firmly in one camp, some in the other, and some will be drawn to both. Each approach uses a particular set of muscles to achieve its end, and each deserves a considered and respectful response.

When I work with writers who generate plot developments as easily as breathing, I genuinely marvel at and celebrate their ability. When I work with writers who savor the intricacies of a complicated character, I settle in for a conversation about that character as if we were discussing a family member. I have more to say about character and plot in Chapters 6 and 7, but for now, give some thought to where you, as teacher and responder, land on this continuum. What's your natural inclination or interest? It's worth knowing, if only to make you aware of your bias.

As a reader, I have been most drawn to character-driven stories, finely nuanced studies of personality, loaded with insight and psychological acuity. Those were the stories I wanted to write, as well.

My early stories and novels were all character driven, tracing the emotional journeys of their main characters. Plot only interested me to the extent that it would reveal my characters and move them forward on whatever emotional journeys they were taking.

For years, I was a character-driven story snob. I considered them the only ones worth writing and the most satisfying stories to read. After a number of years of writing such stories, though, I felt drawn to the challenge of writing a more action-based story. I was encouraged to do this by my son, David (he of the "turn them all into vampires" suggestion).

"You should write a book I'd like," he told me.

"Like what?" I said.

"You know, a book where something happens."

"Stuff happens in my books," I answered. Defensively.

"No, Mom. I mean like on every page."

On every page! The thought was horrifying to me. It was all I could do to move my characters from the dining room to the living room, and here was a call to action on every page. I took the challenge, though, and boy, was I challenged. Now that I've written a few books that are more adventurous romps than emotional journeys I have come around to just how hard they are to pull off.

Over-the-Topness, the ×25 Rule, and Painting with Broad Brushstrokes

I could never have made the switch from writing character-based stories to plot-driven stories without the help of my fiction editor, Stephen Roxburgh. Stephen knows more about how stories work and how to make good books than anyone I know, and he is supremely well versed in the tried-and-true conventions of plot-based stories.

(He was Roald Dahl's editor for *Matilda* and *The BFG*, among others.) Among the myriad of things Stephen taught me, two stand out as touchstones I return to whenever I'm working on stories with plots of action. The first has to do with creating a tone and settling on a consistent level of exaggeration or, what I call, over-the-topness.

My middle-grade novel *The Big House* (2004) opens with a scene in which young Ray and Ivy Fitts attend the trial, conviction, and sentencing of their ne'er-do-well parents, Carol and Dan. The tone, setting, and descriptions are all larger-than-life. The story is hardly realistic and yet not fantasy—more of an entertaining romp. In the initial draft of the opening chapter, the judge sentenced the parents to one year in prison. I wanted a dramatic end to the trial that would whisk the parents offstage and leave the children facing a big challenge. Stephen liked the chapter but commented, "Only *one* year? Why not twenty-five?" Of course! Ramping up the punishment by a factor of 25 instantly upped the ante, increased the stakes, and demanded a correspondingly bigger response from Ivy. Also, a sentence of twenty-five years is just funnier than one year! The lesson made a real impression on me.

I fell back on the "×25" rule time and time again as I crafted the rest of the story. It reminded me to keep the actions and reactions big, broad, and over-the-top. I had to resist my normal inclination toward a subdued plot and spare and understated writing. I was in new territory and had to adapt.

The other essential lesson I learned in writing *The Big House*; its sequel, *Sneaking Suspicions* (2007); and *The Memory Bank* (2010) is that when it comes to characterization it's all right to paint with broad brushstrokes. Characters are revealed through a few defining character traits evident throughout the unfolding action, and they need not change over the course of the story although their circumstances certainly do.

In *The Big House* and *Sneaking Suspicions*, Ivy and Ray are who they are from beginning to end: Ivy the bossy know-it-all older sister, and Ray her loyal and obliging sidekick. The essential dynamic of their truly loving and playful relationship—Ivy declaring what's what (and often being wrong) and Ray asking a lot of good questions but always going along with Ivy—plays out in every scenario. Their relationship dynamic is actually more important to the story than either of them as separate characters.

I always encourage young writers to think about the dominant character traits of their characters and to understand the emotional dynamic of relationships within their stories. In highly imagined, action-filled stories, those dominant traits may be as far as the writer needs to go in fleshing out a character. I also encourage writers of plot-based stories to consider how over-the-top they want them to be and talk to them about the level of magnification necessary to achieve a consistent tone. Does the story need to be ramped up or reined in? In any case, action-based stories deserve to be considered on their own terms and not asked to be something they are not: nuanced character studies or an emotional journey. Plots of action and plots of character are different animals, each valid and deserving of respect.

Know Your Tendencies

Writing a good story of any kind is hard work and takes practice. It helps to know what *kind* of story you're after, though, and this basic distinction between character-driven and plot-driven stories can be informative. As a writer, it reminds me what's most important, what to emphasize, which prize to keep my eyes on. As a teacher, it gives me an overview for responding to a student's story. Having identified what kind of story it is (or clearly wants to be), I can confer with the author about the particular demands of that choice. If the story is action based, then the episodes had better be distinct and exciting and the tension ratcheted up to keep the story moving. If the story centers on a character, then I want to really know and understand the character, what he or she is up against, and how he or she changes over the course of the story.

I often urge my students (of all ages) to know their inclinations and tendencies: to be aware of what comes naturally to them and what they resist; to acknowledge the kinds of stories that appeal most to them; to figure out what helps them to write better stories and what gets in the way. They don't have to do that work all on their own, though. As teachers, we can help them by pointing out what we observe of their process, tastes, and tendencies.

Certainly, a big part of teaching writing involves encouraging young writers to exercise muscles they aren't naturally inclined to use. Writers who are solidly in the character-driven camp usually have to spend more time and effort on the plot of their stories— what happens—and plot-driven writers have to spend more time and energy figuring out what's at stake for their characters. Our work is often to encourage our students to do what doesn't come naturally or feel comfortable or particularly interest them. We can and should acknowledge how hard and counterintuitive it can feel to locate and flex muscles we didn't even know we had. We can also promise that the end result will be satisfying stories that generate interest and heartfelt response.

I wish I had been told about this distinction between character-driven and plot-driven stories when I was younger. I would have understood it. It's not that hard to get. It would have given me a conscious way to look at stories, including my own, earlier on.

CONVERSATIONS AND EXERCISES FOR UNDERSTANDING CHARACTER- VERSUS PLOT-DRIVEN STORIES

- Getting students to name their favorite books, movies, and TV shows can lead to a nonstop avalanche of popular culture overkill. It can also, when reined in, naturally lead into a discussion of character- versus action-driven stories. The kinds of stories that appeal to us reveal things about us and may speak to the kinds of stories we want to write. Have your students decide which end of the continuum their favorite book, movie, or TV show falls on.

- For those who identify an action-based story, have them choose the single most exciting event of the story and talk about what exactly made it exciting—the details, images, and way of presenting it. Ask them to describe how the main character acted and responded. This conversation may help them not to lose sight of their own characters when writing their own climactic scenes.

- For those students who list character-driven stories as their favorites, have them name the most important relationship in a chosen story, and talk about its essential dynamic. Ask them to think about—and say in a sentence or two—how the main character changes over the course of the story.

- Connect these and similar conversations about the stories they read and watch to the stories they write.

Part Two

STORY ELEMENTS

Chapter 5

GATHERING INGREDIENTS

I often use a basic interview/questionnaire to show students that they hold within them the ingredients for many, many stories. Be sure to tell your young writers that it's impossible to fail or do poorly on this exercise. Everyone's answers are right. No one has to share their answers with anyone else if they don't want to. You fill it out, too, along with them. If you decide to use this questionnaire, or some variation of it, please be sure to read the section following it, which elaborates on ways to connect it to story writing.

Adapt this questionnaire in any way that makes it more accessible to your students. Rephrase the prompts, make up categories of your own, get rid of the ones that don't apply. You know your students. Make it longer or shorter, depending on how much time you've got and considering your students' attention spans. If you're comfortable doing so, share some of your own answers to show them that what you're asking is no big deal and that these aren't trick questions. Everything you say will be right, too.

The Questionnaire

■ People

Write the names of three to five people you find interesting, for whatever reason, or three to five people you know really well. Your choices might include family members, friends, siblings, neighbors, or characters in the news or in favorite stories. Write the names of several people you *don't* know well but would like to.

■ Character Traits

Choose one (or more) of your listed people and name the trait that is strongest in that person. Bossy? Funny? Grouchy? Smart? What's the word that best describes that person?

List three animals you know and care about.

Name the dominant character trait of one of those animals.

■ Voices

Name three to five people whose voices you know so well that you can actually hear them inside your head—it's often a family member, close friend, or, sometimes, a teacher. It may or may not be some of the same people already listed. The main thing to think about is the sound of their voice.

■ Expressions

Think about family members, friends, and teachers or characters in stories who say things in a particular way. Perhaps instead of saying *Thank you* they say *Thanks a million* or instead of saying *I love you* they say *Love you to pieces* or perhaps when they are surprised they say *What in Sam Hill*! Take time to think of people and to remember some of the funny, quirky, particular things they say, and then write down a few of those expressions.

■ Gestures

Think of some gestures that you associate with people you know or have observed. Hand-wringing? Knuckle-cracking? Earlobe-pulling? What's a physical tic you're inclined to use when you're nervous or excited? Take a minute to write down a phrase (or draw a picture) that reminds you of a particular gesture you see in your mind's eye.

■ Things That Happened

Think of three different things that happened to you or to people you know that made a big impression on you—events that scared, confused, or surprised you or made you really happy. Times you hold a strong memory of. Perhaps a trip you took, an accident that happened, or when you accomplished something you had never been able to do before. Remember the incident and jot down a few key words that will remind you, not the entire story!

■ Settings

Write down every place—address, town or city, state or country—you have lived. List three to five places, big or small, near or far, that you know well, that you can picture perfectly when you close your eyes.

Write down an imaginary place you would like to visit.

Name a scary place, a safe place, a secret place.

■ Details

Choose several of the places you have listed and write down a specific detail about that place. Is there a particular smell? Are there huge dust bunnies under the bed? Is the house painted the color of mustard? Write down something specific about each place—a chosen detail.

■ Objects

List three to five things—objects, possessions—that mean something to you. Perhaps a special gift you have received or given, something that is valued in your family, or a favorite object you own or wish you had.

■ Images

List three visual images that are plastered in your mind—pictures you can conjure up at will or that come to you unbidden, as in a dream, that are strong and clear.

■ Notions, Ideas, Beliefs

List three things that you wonder about.

List three things you don't understand.

List three things you believe in.

Sharing and Responding to Questionnaires

Writers of all ages usually respond without pain or too much diffi-
culty to this kind of questionnaire, summoning answers and examples from their own lives, things and people and places that have
some meaning to them. In doing so, they gather the main ingredients of story: characters, setting, voices, thematic material, and plot
lines.

Most kids like to share their answers, and you can have a really
good time going over the lists. As they offer their brilliant, funny,
interesting answers, it's the perfect time to make the link between
what they have come up with and how it corresponds to a story element, such as character, plot, setting, and so forth. For instance,
hearing the names of various people and animals students have
listed allows you to point out that they have given themselves a list
of possible characters for their stories.

People

Every story has creatures (human or otherwise) who do things and
to whom things happen. Writers write about characters they care
about and are interested in, and your students have just named a
bunch of such creatures on their lists.

They have also listed people whom they *don't* know but would
like to. Perhaps your students could get to know those people by putting them in a story, by imagining who they might be.

Your students probably know things that have happened to the
people or animals they have listed. Pointing that out allows you to
make the natural link between character and plot—neither exists in
a vacuum!

Character Traits

As for the character traits they listed: with whatever word(s) they chose to describe someone, they began the work of knowing a character, burrowing down inside that person to report what makes that person tick, naming a trait that they consider essential. I'll talk more about this phenomenon in Chapter 6, but this is a time to emphasize that the ability to name a dominant or strong character trait is a fundamental part of knowing a character and creating a story.

Ask your students to think of the character trait in action—i.e., to remember a specific moment or example of the person being grouchy or funny or whatever the chosen trait was. By linking the trait to a specific event or behavior, you once again connect character and action. When your students come up with concrete examples that *reveal* the character trait rather than simply name it, they are answering to the old adage, "Show, don't tell."

Voices and Expressions

Now have your students refer to the voices they know so well they can hear them inside their heads and their lists of expressions. Ask volunteers to say/perform some of those expressions in their best imitation of how the real speaker says them. Whenever I do this exercise with young writers, we end up laughing our heads off, because many of the imitations are so dead-on, so filled with emotion and personality. (It's rare that a killer imitation of their teacher isn't part of the mix; be prepared to hear how you sound to them, and what they choose to remember of all the things you've said!) In saying such small snippets, quick expressions, kids convey so much about a person, a personality, an attitude, and everyone easily responds to and gets it.

When your students have successfully rendered a sampling of distinctive and clear voices, you can point out to them that they have just done the very thing that writers seek to do in their stories: use natural-sounding voices for their characters, choosing words and expressions that reveal who they are. The expressions they come up with are the stuff of realistic dialogue.

Gestures

It's a lot of fun for students to act out gestures they listed. Remind them that they can borrow expressions and gestures from people they know and give them to characters they make up. The examples they'll act out will be real, natural, and specific, and those are qualities they want to carry over into their stories. Whenever someone captures a particularly telling gesture—a movement that packs a lot of emotion or attitude—that's the time to jump in and reiterate that certain gestures and types of body language are a wonderful way to *reveal* characters, to show a deep-down true thing about them.

Berry Morgan, the protagonist of my young adult novel *Many Stones* (2000), is weighed down by grief because of the death of her sister and lingering resentment toward her mostly absent father. She responds with anger to almost everything. In the course of creating her character, I came to hear her angry voice, to know her penchant for arguing with her father. I could see her in my mind's eye and had figured out all sorts of things about her daily life and history. Yet it wasn't until a certain gesture presented itself that I felt I really *had* her: in a magazine, I came across a picture of a woman at a spa, stretched out on a massage table with a row of warmed black stones set along her spine. It was an arresting image—the beautiful polished stones artfully arranged down her back—and for some reason, it instantly collided with everything I knew about Berry, even though I had not been consciously thinking of her. Suddenly, I imagined Berry and a small pile of stones in a very different context. I saw her, in deepest isolation and warding off despair, placing a collection of small stones on top of herself—for comfort, for grounding, out of some need she couldn't express. That imagined gesture introduced the first of many stones that appeared in the story and eventually suggested the book's title, all from a gesture I didn't even know I was looking for!

Things That Happened
In volunteering their answers in this category, students will tell you mini-stories, and chances are you'll hear some succinct and interesting ones. Point out that they have, in fact, told a complete story, not just something that happened but something that happened to someone, in a particular setting, with a particular outcome. It's a chance to be on the lookout for chosen events that clearly engage the listeners, elicit questions or comments—a sign that the student has material of interest. It's worth reiterating that one of the fundamental requirements of a good story is that it be interesting.

Settings

In listing various places, your students have gathered a collection of settings in which a story might unfold. They have named places lodged in their hearts and memories, chosen locations with emotional and historical connections and associations. Often, a memory of a special place can be the spark that leads to story.

I have set all my realistic novels in places I've lived or visited because doing so allowed me to describe them with authority. When I was just learning to write stories, it was a relief to have one element—the setting—that I felt sure of as I juggled all the other story parts.

I used my advance for the novel *Many Stones* to travel to South Africa: an act of faith in the mostly unwritten story and in myself as a writer. Although I had done a great deal of preliminary reading and research, I felt I had to travel there to be able to write convincingly about an American tourist's first visit and impressions.

I lived for a while not far from the small town of Stark, New Hampshire, the setting for *What Jamie Saw* (1995). (I chose this location for its name as well as for its isolated setting.) When I had a nearly completed draft of the story, I spent a weekend there, driving and wandering around to make sure the story I had imagined belonged in Stark.

For my novel *Sneaking Suspicions* (2007), in which Ray and Ivy Fitts find themselves up to their eyeballs in alligators, I made a few interesting excursions through the Everglades, led by a helpful guide who knew the waters well. I consider all the trips I take to immerse myself in a particular setting to be part of what I call my "crooked research."

Details

It comes as news to no one who is teaching writing or trying to write that well-chosen and well-placed details can make a huge difference in bringing a story of any kind to life. The call for specific, revealing detail will be a constant refrain in your work with young writers. Make your plea for them to pay greater attention to everything around them. Good examples from their questionnaires show that it's easier to choose and express perfect details when they're attached to something the writer cares about.

Objects

Things! I love that sturdy, down-to-earth word, and I love the difference chosen things (objects) can make in the stories we write. Read your students a fairy tale, or reminisce about the ones you all know, and zero in on the importance of certain objects—the glass slipper, the magic wand, the poison apple. The well-chosen thing can carry real weight in a story. Your students have now begun a list of things that have special meaning to them, that are concrete and specific— a baseball glove, an item of clothing, a picture, a piece of jewelry— and each comes with a certain history attached. Each one of those objects is an invitation to story.

Images

Strong visual images rendered with carefully chosen words can bring a story to life, electrify it. Your students have chosen a few images that impressed them. They have the raw material to work with. The challenge is to capture the images in words that do justice to what they see in their mind's eye. This type of rendering takes practice and time. Some of your students may want to draw or paint the image before writing it. Some visual images are so strong that they recur throughout the story and become part of its pulse.

Notions, Ideas, Beliefs

The answers to these prompts translate to the thematic concerns of a story—the bigger picture, the overarching or underlying ideas that a story addresses. Often kids write revealing, surprising, and powerful responses. Listen carefully to what they are willing to tell you, and perhaps talk about other stories they know that address some of the same concerns. Point out that stories contain larger, deeper meanings, and let them know that the questions and beliefs they have can be brought to life in a story.

This questionnaire—or a variation of it—is a simple way to gather and consider basic story elements. Have your students save their questionnaires for future reference and possible elaboration. Almost any answer on the list can be used as a writing prompt. For now, it's enough that your students have demonstrated that they harbor the basic elements of stories inside themselves.

ADDITIONAL EXERCISES FOR GATHERING MATERIAL

● *Details:* I encourage *you* to think up whatever simple exercises you can devise for your group of young writers that will help them tune in more carefully to sensory detail. A Best Detail of the Day inscribed on the board? A Best Detail collection, illustrated? Ask them to find a favorite detail in the book that they are currently reading. Think of a way that's appropriate for your students and reminds them to listen and look carefully. Making up an exercise is no big deal, but practicing looking and listening is, and this work should carry on throughout the year.

➻ *Gestures:* Body language. It's an interesting term, don't you think? What do your students make of it? What do they think it refers to? It may be a good starting point for a discussion about gestures, tics, and facial expressions and how weaving them into a story can help a writer capture and convey a character or enrich a scene or encounter.

Gestures and expressions are far easier to act out and see than they are to write. It's a real challenge to capture a gesture efficiently and clearly, with just the right words to convey not only the movement but the particular attitude that accompanies it (or that it accompanies).

Have your students act out some of the particular gestures they associate with family members, friends, and, yes, teachers, and perhaps talk a bit about the person who does it and the mood they're in when they do it. Beware. Once again, they will nail you with imitations of your own little tics and habits. Choose one student to act out and repeat a gesture as many times as necessary while the other students attempt to capture the gesture convincingly in words. Be sure to give the writers time to pare down their descriptions to fit the gesture.

Flip the exercise around. Have students write a description of a chosen expression/gesture and read their best effort to the class. Ask a volunteer who has listened to the description to act it out. See how closely the action matches what the writer intended to convey. This physical exercise may help emphasize the importance of each word in conveying information.

Have your students identify gestures, body language, and facial expressions in books they're reading, and then talk about the emotion conveyed through those descriptions.

Chapter 6

CHARACTERS

The questionnaire in Chapter 5 elicited a smattering of story ingredients. Now let's isolate and consider them individually, starting with the main arteries of any story: *character* and *plot*.

Characters are the people—or creatures—who inhabit our stories. Think Peter Rabbit and his family. Characters are the ones who initiate or respond to the things that happen. They interact with the plot. They feel and think. Often, although not always, they change over the course of the story, in response to things that happen along the way. The power of characters to make or break a story cannot be overemphasized. Authors and readers alike need to know who they are and to care about what happens to them.

One of many things I love about writing and responding to stories is getting to think and talk and speculate about who characters are, why they do what they do, what happens to them, and what it all means. Figuring out what makes a character tick is one of the best, most delicious parts of creating a story. Coming to know who characters are, coming to understand why they act the way they do, plunging them into complicated situations and discovering how they make their way through, this always feels like the real and best work of writing fiction. (See, there I go again with my character bias.) For me it is the eternal gift and miracle of writing stories: going inside the head and heart of someone else, someone as different from me as can be—or as close!

I will tell you the way I see and come to characters. Not everything I say applies to what young writers grapple with in writing their stories, but there's nothing that's beyond them. Perhaps what I say will offer different angles from which to respond to their stories and characters.

Characters come into my mind and heart over time. I am drawn to characters who make me feel deeply—make me mad, confuse me, make me wonder, break my heart, stagger me with what they are up against. My characters must fundamentally interest me, and they must have room to grow. I spend a lot of time with them over the course of writing a story, thinking and wondering about them, figuring out who they are and what has happened in their lives, observing them closely. When they are finally willing to speak to me, I listen carefully to the sounds of their voices, and to what they are trying to say.

Some characters appear strong and clear almost from the beginning, yakking away, doing things, asserting themselves into a story. Others hold back, ghost-like, for so long that I despair of ever getting to know them inside out. Sometimes a character comes to me out of nowhere, and I have to go looking for the story of what happens to him or her. Sometimes the plot idea comes first, and I have to wait and see what characters are needed to play it out. As long as

I have something to start with, even a crumb of an idea, I'm grateful, and go from there.

The journey I make in getting to know, understand, and love a character is much like the journey I make in getting to know anyone I love. It is a journey made over time, day by day, sharing experiences (some of which become the plot of the book), observing, learning when to take the lead and when to sit still and wait and see what happens all on its own. When I am first getting to know a character, I often experience a deep shyness. Who is this person and how dare I write about someone I don't even know? It seems the height of presumption, and I usually beg the character's pardon (who often doesn't even have a name or has a name that will change as the story develops). I stick with whomever is emerging, though, and eventually the shyness evaporates.

I think about my characters the way I think about my friends, family, and people I read about in the newspaper. I wonder about them, daydream about them, worry about their situations, talk to them, try to get them to open up to me.

In trying to know and see them clearly, I write about them separate from the story. I write directly to them, asking questions, telling them what I am dying to know about them. (I ask a lot of questions, period. My journal [see Figure 6.1] is filled with questions—to myself as the writer, to my characters, about the story. Everything starts with questions.) I talk about them with my friends. If I'm lucky, I dream about them. I imagine what they look like. I look for pictures and people who remind me of them. I make note of expressions they use, their particular way of speaking, their gestures, their tics. I try not to get impatient (with them or myself) when I don't understand them right away, can't figure out what happens next, or can't hear their voices. It's funny to think how much of this whole,

what is Jamie's emotional journey?
- stunned by sight of Nin being thrown
- falsely secure by move to trailer
- scared by realization about sitting ducks
- anxious about his mother - confused
  about who takes care of whom
- confused by message from school that
  he's "stupid" because he can't spell
- drawn to magic in a deep tug
- frantic about news that Van is back
- brave in the face of danger
- whole and loved despite it all

where does forgetting come in? remembering?
what are the cues for those?

What's his mother's journey?
- scared to death by Van throwing Nin -
a wake-up call of the worst sort, because
she's been in denial up to that point, and
then is startled into reality by her baby

FIGURE 6.1 *Work journal from* What Jamie Saw

complicated process takes place inside my mind. No wonder I am such a daydreamer.

Along the way, as each character emerges to become who he or she is, I borrow a million little traits, tics, stories, and physical attributes I have observed and stored away during my life. My character may look like someone I know, may be a combination of different personality traits I find interesting, may talk like a member of my own family, but ultimately, the character is his or her own person, unique the way we all are. My characters must stand on their own, and I must stand by them. Respect for them is essential, as it is in all aspects of writing.

As with the people in my life, some characters are easier to know and love than others. It's necessary for me to love them because often a story demands that I look at and say hard things. The only way to do that without cruelty or disdain is to understand and empathize with the wide range of humanity.

When a character finally comes alive with a particular voice, manner, and take on the world, it's cause for celebration. That's when characters can really surprise you, when you discover things about them that you hadn't suspected—a sense of humor, an optimism, a passion for fishing—and when the story can take an interesting turn. Once the characters are fully formed, they work *with* me to tell the story the way it needs to be told. At that point, my work becomes listening and recording rather than dreaming up possibilities. What an amazing process it is—a bit of a miracle, definitely a mystery.

Is this all sounding a bit far-fetched? Made-up characters speaking inside a writer's head, taking on a life of their own, directing a story they are part of? It might sound odd and hardly the stuff of a lesson plan, but if you and your students are willing to write, to give time and attention to burrowing inside characters, I promise you will discover things you didn't know you knew about them.

Characters' Emotional Journeys

A key question that eventually arises around character is, Does a character within a given story make an emotional journey, and if so, what is it? Writers and teachers must both address this question, and it's an important concept to introduce in discussion. The notion will move from abstract to concrete as your writers work to figure out the characters' journeys in their own stories. I address this concept more concretely in Chapter 7.

I often don't know my character's emotional journey until I have a draft of the story. That's why I write the draft: to find out what the story wanted to be about in the first place. And sometimes I can't figure out the journey on my own because I am lost in the forest and can't see the trees. Then my fellow writers or my editor help me to see. A big part of our work as teachers is to help writers see what they've got that they might not be aware of—in other words, to help them see inside their stories.

Let me give you some examples of emotional journeys that characters have taken in some of the stories I've written. (I cite my own stories and characters only because they're the ones I can speak of with authority when it comes to process and intention.)

What Jamie Saw (1995) tracks one little boy's emotional journey from fear to a sense of safety. It took me a long time of writing and rewriting the story before that simple underlying premise became clear. Once I finally saw it, the identified emotional journey helped me enormously in revising and directing the story, in knowing what belonged and what did not. Even once I understood the arc I was after with the story—bringing Jamie to a certain sense of safety, beyond the point of danger—I had to follow a very crooked, up-and-down, one-step-forward/two-steps-back map. Characters, like the rest of us, don't move forward in neat, defined, unencumbered trajectories. The basic journey they make is bound to involve a host of detours and accompanying emotional states.

My first novel, *Tell Me Everything* (1993), tracks a twelve-year-old girl's journey from grief to acceptance. Roz (my main character) has lost her mother and is struggling to come to terms with that loss. During the years that I worked on that story, I came to picture Roz's grief as an arrow shot straight from her heart, traveling through time and experience (the scenes and chapters of the book) until finally reaching its target: acceptance. (In my mind, the arrow sunk into a solid, mighty tree with a satisfying *thunk*.) My job as writer was to travel with that arrow, writing down what happened along the way, the stations and moments of Roz's journey.

My intermediate-/middle-grade romps, *The Big House* (2004) and *Sneaking Suspicions* (2007), are plots of action. As I mentioned earlier, the main characters, Ray and Ivy, don't change as the stories unfold. They remain their irrepressible selves and true to their essential dynamic—Ivy as the know-it-all older sister and Ray as her loyal and innocent partner-in-crime—as they move through the paces of their adventures. The challenge in writing these characters was to establish that key dynamic, the deep and abiding affection between them, and to come up with situations that allowed their essential natures to shine. Instead of the stories being guided by Ray and Ivy's emotional journeys, they were guided by solving problems, facing challenges, and clearing up mysteries.

The emotional arc of *The Memory Bank* (2010), my graphic story book with artist Rob Shepperson, starts with the separation of two sisters, Hope and Honey Scroggins, and ends with their reunion. Their separate journeys back to one another are rendered in both pictures and words, and, as in *The Big House* and *Sneaking Suspicions*, the emphasis is less on how the characters change and more on their deep bond and the amazing and magical world they enter when they both leave home.

Why parse all these stories and boil them down to their essential emotional journeys? I'm pointing out the interior map that I came to see, over time, was there, and that guided me in writing them.

Thinking of the clear, simple thing we can say in response to someone else's story is our main job in responding. If we are on the lookout for and can suggest an emotional journey that the character might be taking, we can sometimes help the writer see his or her story's trajectory. Once articulated, that trajectory often becomes easier to write.

DOMINANT CHARACTER TRAITS

In stories where the character does not change, and may be presented in broader, even caricatured style, there is still a need to capture and portray that character in a way that readers can relate to and relish. It is always helpful, I find, for authors to be clear about their primary characters' dominant emotional trait—the characteristic that best defines and reveals them. What is at the heart of them? What makes them tick? Pondering those questions is the work of a writer every bit as much as listening and looking are. Identifying essential character traits and then showing them through action (rather than telling *about* them) is a fundamental part of any writer's journey. In any story, at any age, a writer can practice showing, not telling.

In *The Big House*, Ivy and Ray's character traits create an essential dynamic between them that plays out repeatedly throughout the story. In the following exchange—after villain Marietta has threatened to test the children before sending them off to separate boarding schools—that dynamic is revealed through action and dialogue:

> On their way down to the hideout Ray asked her, "Do we have to take the test?"
>
> Ivy knew what his face looked like even without looking at it: the way he looked when he had to get a shot. "We'll review," she told him. "I'll be the teacher." She'd go over everything she could remember from first and second grade. "Addition and subtraction," she said. She wouldn't bother with spelling, which she'd never had any luck with.
>
> That night, with every message she sent down via the intercom she included a math problem. She made sure to use lots of 11's and 7's, 7 and 11 being known lucky numbers. Ray got three in a row right, and Ivy thought that was a good note on which to end their day.

In discussing the story, I can say that Ivy is bossy and take-charge and will do whatever she can think of to help her brother, even if her grasp of the situation is limited. Little Ray is trusting and vulnerable and goes along with whatever Ivy says. In writing the story, however, I have to *show* those traits in action.

EXERCISES IN SUPPORT OF GETTING TO KNOW CHARACTER

➡ You might initiate and guide a conversation considering what it means "to make an impression" on someone. Ask your students to tell of memorable first impressions that people or animals have made on them, being sure to elicit the details/words/actions that created those strong impressions.

- Ask your students to think about what kind of first impression they want a chosen character to make on the reader. Do they want the reader to like her? Think she's funny? Think he's brave or wretched? Choose a book character or historical figure they all know and generate a list of that person's characteristics. It won't take long for a few basic traits to emerge.

  Once you've settled on the character's strongest traits, ask for specific examples of situations in which the character displayed those dominant traits. This exercise is another opportunity to point out the link between character and plot.

- Tell your students a story about someone you know who changed in some large or small way; maybe this will be a story about yourself. Ask your students to think about changes they have witnessed in someone over time—a change in attitude or ability, level of confidence or kindness, or generosity. Kids with siblings will usually come up with a story pretty quickly. Discuss how hard or easy, slow or fast the journey was, and what steps were taken along the way. Look for definite turning points, moments when it became clear that the person was on a new and different track.

  Now track the emotional journey of a character in a book you have all read, and ask what emotional or psychological state the character starts out in, and what state (changed or not) they end up in. Name the key points along that character's journey. Talk about the process of change within people and characters, and remind your students that characters might start out being one way and end up being changed by what happens to them in the story.

➥ You might ask your students to write a character sketch of someone they know, imagine, or would like to know (but first, please, read Chapter 8). In advance, read aloud a passage from one of the books you are reading in class that you feel does a good job of introducing and describing an interesting character. Ask your students to point out the details that stay with them, that they remember, and figure out, with them, how the author conveyed emotional information about the character through chosen words, details, and descriptions. (If you can't find a good example, grab hold of any of Roald Dahl's stories. He is a master at wonderful and vivid character descriptions.)

In their own sketches, remind students to include specific detail and description, gesture and facial expression. Ask them to think about the single most important character trait they want to convey about that person, and choose fitting events to show that trait in action. This exercise is not a story per se; it need not have a shape or climax or conclusion to it. Basically, this exercise is a variation on the old stand-by assignment to "write about someone you admire," only, in this case, it's "introduce me to someone who, for whatever reason, interests you, and be very clear about what kind of impression you want that person to make on your reader."

Chapter 7

PLOT

ow, for the other main artery of a story: *plot.*

There are plot lovers and plot resisters, but it's a fundamental element of story that all writers must address. I struggled mightily with it and still do.

The bottom line, as far as plot goes, is that *something must happen* in a story—events, actions, exchanges that make sense and are interesting, things a reader can follow and relate to at some level. Some writers struggle with having *too much* happen, and their stories cave beneath the weight and confusion of an unresolved or overly convoluted plot. Other writers, myself included, struggle to make *anything* happen and run the risk of creating stories that are boring or quiet to the point of silence. Striking the right balance, crafting an unfolding plot line that best serves the story each writer wants to tell, that's the challenge.

The essential question that underlies plotting is, *What if?* The writer asks what happens—what *could* happen—and then what happens after that. The chosen incidents are arranged in a way that makes sense and that lead the reader through the story from beginning to end.

To get our bearings with plot, I've chosen yet another beloved creature to guide us: Babar. You know Babar—the wonderful elephant who looks so dashing in his green suit. *The Story of Babar* (1933), by Jean de Brunhoff, is a picture book I show to young writers of all ages when it's time to talk about plot, about all the things that can happen in a story. What happens, and then what happens next—all the events that move a story forward, from beginning to end—are on beautiful display in this book.

Consider, along with your students, what Babar does, what happens to him, in the nonstop unfolding of his story:

He is born.
He is rocked in a hammock by his mother.
He plays with the other elephants; digs in the sand.
His mother is shot by a wicked hunter. (Quite the initiating
    incident.)
He is chased by the hunter.
He runs away.
He comes upon a busy town.
He is befriended by a nice old lady who gives him her purse.
He goes on a shopping spree, kicked off by numerous rides in
    an elevator.
He buys many fine clothes, including a fetching green suit.
He has his portrait taken.
He eats and sleeps, exercises, and takes a bath.

He goes out for a ride in the car that the old lady has given
      him.

He studies and talks about his life in the forest.

He stands at the window thinking of friends and family.

His cousins Arthur and Celeste appear.

He treats them to fine clothes and little cakes at the bakery.

Everyone in the forest searches for Arthur and Celeste.

An old marabou spots them and reports the news.

Arthur's and Celeste's mothers come to town to claim and
      scold them.

Babar decides to return to the forest.

He packs his trunk.

He says good-bye to the old lady and drives off.

Since the old king has eaten a bad mushroom and died,
      Cornelius asks Babar to become king.

Babar reveals he and Celeste are engaged.

Animals are dispatched with invitations for a party to cele-
      brate the marriage and coronation and to buy beautiful
      wedding clothes.

Guests arrive and King Babar, Queen Celeste, and everyone
      dance.

Night falls.

Babar and Celeste take off in a big yellow balloon.

Never a dull moment with Babar! One thing happens and then
another and another, each one with its own emotional charge; each
one pushing the story forward. Some things that happen are big and
bold (his mother is shot by the hunter); some are purely delightful
(Babar's shopping spree, his luck in meeting up with the old lady.
"She gives him whatever he wants" is one of my all-time favorite

lines in children's literature); some are quiet and interior (he thinks of his life in the forest; he misses his mother; night falls). What happens is wide ranging, and there's a corresponding range of emotional responses. Nearly every page spread offers a fine example of a new plot development that creates a certain tone and elicits an emotional response.

I hold up this story as an example of a winning plot, written with both imagination and authority.

Invigorated by Babar, you and your students might begin to think about the plot lines of your own stories, what incidents you have chosen, the order in which they unfold, the extent to which they are—and are not—linked to one another.

Many young writers are comfortable plotting their stories, thinking up things that could happen. Their imaginations are there for them. Let them draw on that ability even as you encourage them to think about *why* something happens when and where it does in a story and how it affects the main character. By wondering about those connections, they will start to stitch together all the threads that make up a story.

Plot Intersecting with Character

Thinking about plot inevitably leads to thinking about character, because the things that happen involve the main characters.

In my character-driven stories, what happens is primarily determined by where my character is in his or her emotional journey. I work backward from the emotional arc of the story (once I've figured out what it is) to come up with the necessary plot developments. I ask, what needs to happen at this point in the story to bring my character to this particular stage in his or her emotional journey?

In more action-based stories, the episodes are not as tied to or dependent on the character's emotional state, although there is always a connection between what is happening and the main character. In *The Memory Bank* (2010), which Rob Shepperson and I created in collaboration, many of the episodes grew out of our enthusiasm for our imagined places and contraptions: a memory bank where all the memories in the world are sorted and stored, a dream vault where dreams are gathered in small leather pouches and preserved in a celestial ceiling, a memory dump where so-called broken memories are discarded. We had a great time creating imaginary places and wild characters to play around in them. In revision, we had to make sure the various episodes connected with the ongoing emotional journey of our main characters, Hope and Honey.

Storyboarding

I want to devote the rest of this chapter on plot to a storyboarding exercise I came up with many years ago when I was writing short stories and needed a simple way to focus on what was—or wasn't—happening in them.

This exercise has its roots in comic books, specifically the old Uncle Scrooge (Barks 1987) comic books, which both my children read fairly obsessively (and which clearly helped them learn to read). As I was oh so slowly grappling with writing scenes, trying to build tension and see the overall shape of my story and get from the beginning to the end, my daughter was poring over delightful tales made with a few chosen words and pictures, with bubbles for the dialogue, a line or two of text at the bottom of every square to move the narrative along, an occasional flashback quickly revealed in the corner of the panel. In short, everything I was trying to do in a simplified and graphic form. I, who cannot draw to save my life, took note, and grabbed a piece of blank paper and started to map out the story I'd been working on: a square for each scene; a stick-figure image to illustrate it; a phrase at the bottom saying the main thing that happened in the scene. Later, as I came to more deeply understand that connection between plot and character, I added the dominant emotion of the main character to track the emotional arc of the story along with its unfolding plot.

This exercise calls on the writer to think of a story in terms of the main things that happen within it, beginning to end, and to ask three questions of each scene or section along the way.

1. What is the main thing that happens in this part of the story?
2. What is the strongest visual image in this part of the story? (Another way of asking this is, When I picture this part of the story inside my head, what do I see?)
3. What is the dominant emotion in this part of the story?

In answering each of these three questions, the writer will create a storyboard with a square for each main scene and include

- a phrase or simple sentence stating the main thing that happens;
- a simple drawing to illustrate the strongest visual image; and
- a word for the dominant emotion of the main character.

With beginning writers, I often start with this prompt: "Think of something that happened to you when you were little. Something that made an impression on you—scared you, made you happy, surprised you, something you thought was so funny." That's all you need to say. By this time, everyone has something in mind. *First thought, best thought* works like a charm, as far as this exercise goes.

I'm including my own storyboard answer to this prompt so you can see the simplicity of exactly what I'm talking about (Figure 7.1).

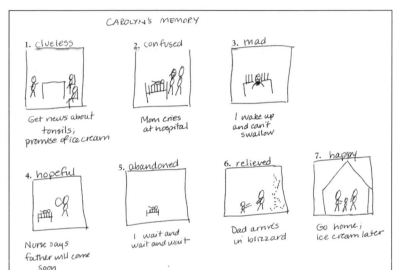

Square 1: When I was a kid, I got lots of awful ear-aches. Finally, when I was six years old, the doctor said I had to have my tonsils taken out. I didn't know what an operation was, but the doctor told me that after the operation I could eat all the ice cream I wanted, so I was interested.

Square 2: My parents took me to the hospital for the operation. When my mother kissed me good-bye, I saw that she was crying.

Square 3: When I woke up from the operation, my throat hurt so much that I couldn't swallow, much less eat anything, not even ice cream. Why had the doctor lied to me? Did he think I wouldn't notice how much my throat hurt?

Square 4: The nurse told me that my father would come to take me home soon.

Square 5: I waited and waited and waited in my hospital bed, and no one came and I thought no one ever would.

Square 6: Finally, my father appeared and told me that Chicago had been hit by a terrible blizzard! That's what had taken him so long! Why hadn't the nurse just told me?

Square 7: Dad and I got home, and Mom was waiting. After awhile, I felt well enough to eat ice cream.

A simple story about having my tonsils out when I was six. A tiny emotional journey that started with anticipation of promised ice cream and ended with delivery of that promise, with disillusionment and feeling abandoned in between!

FIGURE 7.1 *Carolyn's storyboard #1*

To introduce the exercise to your students, perhaps you can create a storyboard of your own, on the board or on a large sheet of paper, to show them how it's done. (They'll also like hearing about something that happened to you when you were a kid.) Don't worry if, like me, you cannot draw. Your effort will reinforce that the exercise does not require artistic talent in order to be helpful.

Now ask your students to break down the story they have in mind to the main events that happened along the way, beginning to end. Using a piece of paper divided into six to eight squares (or a patch of blackboard or on a sketch pad on an easel) have them write down in one phrase or sentence the main thing that happens—or the main thing the main character *does*—scene by scene. Ask them to sketch a simple picture of the visual image they have for each scene or moment. Finally, ask them to name the dominant emotion of the main character in each scene.

I usually ask three volunteers to come to the front of the classroom to do their storyboards as the others work on theirs at their desks. This exercise can be helpful whether or not the writer is a gifted artist, but it offers artistic students a chance to shine. When everyone is finished (ten minutes is usually enough time for most to complete their work) have the volunteers tell their stories, relying on and referring to the blocks of their storyboards as they do so.

The exercise is as simple as can be and certainly not original. I use this co-opted storyboard technique to distill short stories and novels and to track both the unfolding action and emotional changes of the main character.

I include a storyboard for my novel *What Jamie Saw* (1995) so you can see how this exercise can be adapted for longer stories as well (Figure 7.2). Each block represents a chapter of the complete novel, reduced to its essential action and emotion.

FIGURE 7.2 Carolyn's storyboard #2

For a long time, I was embarrassed that I even used this technique. I still labored under the impression that "real writers" would never resort to such explicit distillation of a story, could somehow hold the whole thing in their heads without trying to lay it out on a single page. When I finally started using the exercise in fiction-writing classes, I half expected some administrator to knock on the door and haul me off, exposing me for the impostor I was.

It never happened. I've demonstrated this storyboarding technique many times over the years, to writers of all ages, and had them try it—at their desks, up at the board, using big easels at workshops. It's extremely flexible. I've given hours-long presentations on storyboarding and demonstrated it as a mini-lesson. You can extend it as long as you like or condense it to fit whatever time period you must answer to. Inevitably, writers offer up interesting stories, draw revealing little sketches, and jump into raw emotional content.

Responding to Storyboards

It's rare that these storyboard exercises aren't satisfying. They're concise and chosen stories that matter to the writer/illustrator. This exercise once again gives you the opportunity to point out all the aspects of story that your writers attended to naturally, without thinking or worrying about it. They came up with a story idea and chose material that mattered to them. They started it somewhere (the beginning) and moved the narrative forward (the sequential squares or scenes). They tracked an emotional journey as well, by identifying the dominant—and probably changing—emotions of the protagonist. They built the story out of episodes/moments/scenes connected to one another and worked toward a climax or turning point. Most of their storyboards will contain an identifiable beginning, middle, and end—no small feat! Each story will be told from a distinct point of view (usually the author's own, but it still gives you the chance to introduce the concept, and doing so in reference to his or her own story can make a strong impression on the writer). The story will also have a certain tone you can affirm. It may be funny, scary, sad, or surprising. Almost all the stories will naturally contain a narrative arc. Here's your chance to identify it and applaud your writers for having incorporated it!

A key point regarding the stories is the linkage from scene to scene. Sometimes I ask the writers to add a plus (+) sign between the scenes to emphasize their connection, that they *build* on one another to add up to create the entire story. It's a quick, simple, visual way to make the point that no scene exists in a vacuum. They are all tied together; they accumulate. When a writer is working on a new story, trying to figure out what happens next, he or she needs to be aware that whatever happens must link up with, connect to, make sense according to what has happened before and what will happen afterward as well.

Aside from the basic elements of storytelling, there is always plenty to comment on in considering the individual storyboards. I typically go by what strikes me first—the thing about the story that grabs me. It can be anything from a particularly striking picture to a particularly clear and concise statement of something that happens to a particularly dramatic climax. There is always something of interest to comment on. When questions pop up—and they inevitably do—the writer is always capable of answering because he or she knows this story well, inside and out.

SCENES

Reviewing storyboards naturally leads to considering scenes in a story. Scenes are distinct units, or building blocks, part of a bigger story but also with a life of their own. Often they take place in a time or place that distinguishes them from other scenes of the story, and each one contains a distinct event, exchange, or action that moves the story forward. Scenes are probably my favorite building block: short enough to be manageable and yet often emerging as mini-stories themselves. Learning how to write a good scene (and glory be, it *can* be learned) sets a writer on his or her way to writing a whole story or novel. Dealing with a contained scene is not as daunting as looking at an entire story or novel. It's one small piece. Have your students concentrate on writing good, solid scenes one at a time. With enough of them strung together in the right way and in the right sequence, your writers will hold complete stories in their hands.

You can return again and again to the key questions: What's the main thing that happens in this scene? What's the dominant emotion of this scene? Both need to be rendered. Who are the characters in it, and what do they do and say? From whose point of view is the scene told? In asking these questions, you point out that writing a scene addresses matters of narration, setting, dialogue, and plot development.

Have your students identify a definite and clear-cut scene from their storyboards. Ask them to identify its beginning, middle, and ending, and then have them write that scene alone. It will be short and contained and yet call on them to exercise some essential storytelling muscles.

USE OF STORYBOARDS DURING DRAFTING AND REVISION

The storyboard exercise based on a childhood memory is a simple way to introduce and demonstrate plot and how it unfolds in a story and to track the emotional arc. In responding to this memory/story, you can emphasize identifying story elements even as you appreciate the chosen memory.

Once writers have begun crafting their own stories, creating and revising drafts, storyboards can once again be a useful tool. Reducing drafts into storyboards lets writers see what they've got, beginning to end, in a simple, graphic form. They can reveal trouble spots and serve as maps for future revision. It's appropriate to respond to storyboards that are based on stories-in-progress with more questions and attention to the story. Here are some considerations and questions that frequently come up when I go over my students' storyboards.

Main Thing That Happens

Reducing to a phrase the main thing that happens in a scene or chapter of a story is an exercise in discriminating and prioritizing. When I first started using storyboards for the short stories I was working on, I often found I couldn't come up with any phrase at all—because *nothing happened!* I often just had characters talking or thinking, scene after scene. The storyboard made clear to me the places in my story that were redundant or where nothing was happening and held me accountable to the fact that something (however small or subtle) *must* happen. For writers who suffer from an overabundance of things happening, this exercise forces them to choose and name the most important thing. In revision, that chosen action deserves the greatest attention and focus. Do the scenes (or chapters) unfold in an order that makes sense and that builds tension? Sometimes the storyboard can point out a need to shuffle certain scenes, to change the sequence to achieve a smoother flow.

Illustrations

Marks of all kinds reveal things. Look for the relative size of the characters. Look for the space between characters and around them. Look for a particular visual detail the student may have included, signaling its importance. Look for illustrations that differ from what is described in the text. Are there repeating images? Do the repetitions signal redundancy in the story or the importance of a certain image? Look for visual clues about the story; they will be there no matter how rough and simple the drawings may be. What do other students notice in the drawings? What does the artist see? Were there any surprises?

Emotional Tracking

Although I initially used storyboarding to help me with plotting—to make sure that something was happening in every scene—I quickly came to rely on it as a way of tracking the emotional arc of the story. Naming the dominant emotion of the main character from scene to scene gives the writer a quick way to follow the character's emotional journey and to see whether it makes emotional sense. This consideration is especially important in a character-driven story where the emphasis is on the emotional or interior life of the character and how that character changes over time.

Look at the emotions your young writers have identified in their storyboards, and talk about the ways in which they change according to what is happening. Talk about the emotional state a character starts out in, the state that character ends up in, and all the steps along the way. Over time, your young writers will grow accustomed to thinking about the emotional arcs of their stories. You can also remind them that in the written story their identified emotions need to be revealed through action, gesture, detail, nuance: *show, don't tell*.

When I write stories, I am constantly asking myself where my character is emotionally, how or what he or she is feeling inside, regardless of words or actions—how he or she *really* feels. That emotion, that bottom-line emotion, is the one that needs to come across in the story, both in how it's written and in what happens. So figuring out and naming the dominant emotion matters in getting the story right and keeping it on track. Getting students to track emotional development is a little bit like asking them to watch their thinking. It's another invitation to them to pay attention, to be interior detectives.

The identified dominant emotion must change from scene to scene, if only incrementally, and must progress in a believable way (in much the same way that the plot developments must change and connect to one another in a believable way).

I've read plenty of student stories in which a character erupts in anger and then, moments later, drifts off into sweet slumber. Really? To go from extreme agitation to a delicious nap? Not physiologically true. Not the way our minds and bodies work together. The character might well go to sleep at some point in the story, but there are probably a few emotional states and steps between the outburst and repose.

Another problem a storyboard can point out is an unchanging emotional state—the character is only mad all the time or only confused from beginning to end. Sometimes when I do a storyboard, I discover that I've written several scenes that emphasize a certain emotional state repeatedly. Being able to see an overview allows me to catch the redundancies and identify places that can be edited. If I have repeating scenes, then my job is to pick the best one.

Interior, emotional, psychological changes never—or rarely—follow a smooth and logical path. Emotions go up and down. We advance and retreat. Two steps forward, one step back. But we get there; we change. Stories tell us about that, and it's one of the main reasons we love them.

Chapter 8

VOICES AND DIALOGUE

Plot and *character* may be the main arteries of the story, the essential ingredients, but there are other related story elements that are terrifically important as well.

At the top of my list come the voices that speak within the story. I'm talking about voices, plural, as distinct from what is sometimes referred to as the story's—or writer's—"voice," which is often linked to the voice of the narrator. This is an important distinction, but not one I want to address here. In terms of working with young writers, I think the emphasis should stay on how the voices of their chosen characters sound.

So let's start with the basics. Characters speak. They need to have voices that are as unique as they are. Everyone who speaks in a story should sound distinct, just the way the people we know have their own way of talking, their own rhythms, tone, and particular way of saying things.

Let's revisit Peter Rabbit and find the voices there—who actually speaks and how they sound. Surprisingly, only Mrs. Rabbit and Mr. McGregor—not Peter—have words to say. First, Mrs. Rabbit:

"'Now, my dears,' said old Mrs. Rabbit one morning, 'you may go into the fields or down the lane, but don't go into Mr. McGregor's garden: your father had an accident there; he was put in a pie by Mrs. McGregor.'" Her few words pack quite a punch, don't they? Consider how much is revealed: we hear the words of a loving mother, calling her children "dears" and looking out for their safety. She is also no-nonsense, revealing crucial information and scary history in a particular way. Skipping over any gruesome details, she still neatly and economically captures the life and death consequences: "He was put in a pie." She finishes by saying, "Now run along and don't get into mischief. I'm going out." She offers the classic charge of mothers everywhere and throughout time, but in her own particular way. She doesn't say, "be good" or "stay out of trouble." She says, "don't get into mischief." Every word in a story, including every word of dialogue, is an act of choice. Having issued the warning and revealed the sad history, she takes her leave, joining literature's many other parents and grown-ups who must exit the scene so that the children's adventure can commence! Mrs. Rabbit is heard from again, at the end, as she administers Peter's medicine: "One tablespoon to be taken at bedtime." Her voice is consistently in-charge, no-nonsense, protective, and clear.

Mr. McGregor's spoken words are few indeed: "Stop Thief!" But they're plenty! No more *needs* to be said. The use of the word "thief" and the command to "stop" make clear that Mr. McGregor is angry, views Peter as a trespasser, and means to catch him. With the memory of Peter's father "put in a pie" fresh in the reader's mind, and with the wonderful accompanying pictures, those two words, "Stop Thief," say it all. They are pared down to bare bones. We hear a distinct and insistent voice cry out in a short burst that propels the story forward and does nothing to get in the way of its continuing. The tension level ratchets higher, and action ensues.

So much for the voices in *The Tale of Peter Rabbit* (1902). What about the voices in your stories, in your students' stories? Are they natural sounding and distinct? Do they say enough, too much, or too little? Do they sound just the way they should?

I love encouraging writers to train their ears to listen for the wonderful expressions and rhythms of the speech around them, in the stories they read, watch, and listen to. I try to make them aware of the voices they have already embedded in their minds and hearts, to call on them and run with them in the stories they write.

Referring to the questionnaire in Chapter 5 in which students listed voices and expressions they know well, remind your students that they already harbor a number of voices in their hearts and memories. You may need to remind them again and again, because the natural ability to remember and imitate real-sounding voices often goes into hiding as soon as young writers put pen to paper.

Years ago I visited a second-grade classroom, and a student showed me a poem she had written about a "lad and lassie." She explained to me that those words meant boy and girl. When I asked her why she didn't just use the words *boy* and *girl*, she told me, wide eyed, "I can't do that. This is *poetry*!" At age seven, she already had such a strong and certain notion that writing (in this case, poetry) demanded a different vocabulary, a fancier way of expression. Many beginning writers (of any age) operate from similar interior constraints, basically that the words we know and use, the voices that surround us and fill our heads, probably aren't "good enough" for real writing. People in stories need somehow to sound better, smarter, or more articulate than we are. But no, they don't. They need to sound like who they are. They need to sound believable, natural, distinct, and appropriate to the story they inhabit. If only the lad and lassie had been playing on a moor!

LISTENING

My first published book, *Body and Soul* (1988), was an adult, nonfiction collection of interviews that I worked on in collaboration with photographer Judy Dater. We traveled around the country meeting women who had interesting and widely different backgrounds, experiences, and outlooks. I tape-recorded our interview sessions and then transcribed them, editing and resequencing the women's words to tell their own stories. This work of oral history and nonfiction did more to help me develop as a fiction writer than any other project. First, it impressed on me the need for a shape to each story—beginning, middle, and end. It also taught me a great deal about the importance and beauty of each person's distinct voice.

Initially, I found transcribing the tapes to be a fairly tedious duty, but it quickly became clear that listening to the recording over and over again as I transcribed each woman's words allowed the rhythm, cadence, chosen expressions, and timbre of her voice to flow inside me. That exercise in repeated listening helped me incorporate all their voices. Over the course of compiling their stories, I came to hear their voices *inside* me—a standard that I now set for the characters in my novels. I need to be able to hear their voices before I trust that their voices are believable and natural sounding.

DIALOGUE

Dialogue is the writer's chance to bring natural-sounding, distinct voices together in natural-sounding conversations, in exchanges that are appropriate to who the characters are and how they speak and interact. Good dialogue is enormously satisfying.

Dialogue is also a chance to reveal character and move the story forward. Many beginning writers waste dialogue on boring back-and-forth exchanges, saying things that don't really matter to the story, that don't reveal anything about the character, or that reveal information better told in straightforward exposition.

Emerging writers also tend to generate much more dialogue than is actually needed in the story. However, often within a bunch of dialogue that *isn't* necessary or revealing lurk a few perfect lines that capture the distinct sound of someone's voice and the exact way two (or more) characters speak and respond to one another. As teachers and readers, we need to be able to identify these perfect lines, to extract and praise them, to show how they convey what is essential.

Some key questions in generating and responding to dialogue are: Is this exchange of dialogue necessary? Do the speakers sound natural and consistent? Does what they have to say to each other reveal who they are or move the story forward? Do they reveal information in a way that is believable and natural sounding? What are the best lines? Can any of the other lines be cut and not be missed?

TONE AND EMOTION

Dialogue can go a long way in setting the emotional tone of a scene or chapter and in revealing the essence of a character or a relationship dynamic. The *way* characters speak to one another conveys a great deal, regardless of *what* they are speaking about. Here's an example from my young adult novel *Many Stones* (2000), chock-full of the anger and tension that permeate the father–daughter relationship at the heart of this story:

> My father returns after about an hour. I haven't moved off the bed. "Call home?" he asks.
>
> "Yeah," I tell him. "I called Josh."
>
> "Josh?" I can hear how wrong, wrong, wrong my answer is. Dad has met Josh twice and obviously thinks he is a loser.
>
> "Yeah," I say. "Josh."
>
> He comes to stand in the doorway of my room. He is such a big man. His shoes are very soft leather. "You called Josh?" he repeats.
>
> I wonder how many times we can go back and forth saying Josh's name, which one of us will give up first. I do. "Yes," I say. But then I change my mind and add, "Josh."
>
> He purses his lips and considers what he is going to say next. "Berry, when I suggested calling home, it wasn't Josh I had in mind."
>
> I don't miss a beat. "Then when *you* call home, don't call Josh." (49–50)

What Berry and her father are talking about in this exchange does not really matter. What matters is how they speak to each other and the reservoir of anger they bring to the conversation.

Every word a character speaks, and every exchange between characters, affects the emotional tone and has room for emotional undercurrents. The sooner young writers become aware of that possibility, the sooner they can write a more powerful story.

TAGS

Tags—identifying who is saying what—make for a solid mini-lesson from time to time. Their importance is clear. The reader needs to know who is speaking in a story in order not to be confused. *He said, she said* are simple tags that clarify (and an opportunity for you to jump in with some basic rules regarding punctuation). When a character speaks, leading or ending with *she said* or naming the character, as in *John said,* will do the trick. Of course, you can quickly accumulate too many *saids,* and then, in revision, it's time to consider which ones are needed and which can be cut. If it's absolutely clear who is speaking, then no tag is needed. There are also variations on ways to identify who is speaking. Try using other words: *told, asked, answered.* Often the character speaking is identified by the line that follows, that is, *"I don't want to go." Mary pinched her mouth in a pouty frown.*

Many beginning writers of all ages attach an adverb—*she said, angrily*—to spoken words to convey a certain emotional state. The impulse to reveal emotion is correct, but the spoken words, along with specific gestures and details, do a better job of showing how the character is feeling. In general, adverbs are suspect. However, those first-draft adverbs are a clue for the writer, identifying places that need, in revision, to show rather than tell how their characters are feeling. First drafts usually offer up a bunch of places where the author can, in revision, "show, not tell."

The young writer should concentrate on identifying the speaker for clarity's sake, and if need be, in revision, cut redundancies or introduce other ways of identifying the speaker. *He said/she said* is the simple answer to fall back on until they are comfortable with the nuances of capturing dialogue, and their real attention should go to what the characters are actually saying. If they lead with vibrant, distinct voices, the tags will take their rightful place, disappearing into the background.

Once your students are grappling with dialogue in their own stories, ask them to consider an exchange of dialogue in their current favorite book to identify the various tags the author used.

EXERCISES IN SUPPORT OF LISTENING FOR AND COMING TO KNOW PARTICULAR VOICES

I've used these exercises with my adult students in various fiction-writing classes, and they can be adapted to work with students of all ages. Fiddle with them in any way you want to make them accessible.

◆◆ *Oral History:* Have your students ask a family member to tell them a family story and, if possible, record that conversation. Have your students play back the recording and transcribe their favorite sections. Ask them to underline the sentences that sound the most like the speaker, the lines the interviewer particularly remembers the speaker saying. Perhaps ask the student to imitate exactly how the person spoke them. This is an exercise not only in recording oral history but also in listening and transcribing, adding another voice to the repertoire of voices they hold inside—a repertoire they can draw from when they write stories of their own.

➤ *An Eavesdropping Exercise:* Most writers are incorrigible eavesdroppers. There is so much to recommend eavesdropping: the lure of someone else's story, an intimate dialogue, an intriguing-sounding voice. Listening to others speak is a good way to train the ear to pay attention, to take note of detail.

This exercise zeros in on both the sounds of voices and the rhythms of dialogue. Have your students eavesdrop on a conversation (or merely listen as a conversation between two people takes place in front of them, without taking part in it themselves). They're not to write anything down—yet. The whole point is for them to listen intently, to let words and phrases imprint on their minds. When the conversation is over, that's when your students write down as much of the back-and-forth as they can remember— the exact phrases and words (and *only* the spoken words—no tags, gestures, or details woven in). You want them, to the best of their ability, to replay the dialogue in their memory, to hear the voices again inside their head as they write down what people said. Ask them to underline the single expression, phrase, or sentence that they like best, that they remember most clearly, that somehow captures the voice they overheard. Have students read their overheard exchanges aloud. After a number of exercises have been read, ask your students what lines linger with them. There will be clear favorites—a chance to point out that certain ways of saying things make an impression and convey a lot. Identifying the best snippets makes the point that a little can go a long way in establishing a distinct voice. If nothing else, this exercise always offers up great lines.

• *Monologues:* Ask your students to write a short monologue using one of the voices they listed on their questionnaire from Chapter 5—a voice they know so well they can hear it inside their heads. Ask them to write a paragraph or a page or more of their chosen person speaking about something he or she would naturally choose to speak about. This ends up being an exercise not only in voice but also in first-person narration: "I" speaks. Let's say your student chooses the voice of Aunt Sally, someone who loves to go bowling. Have your student pretend that he or she is Aunt Sally talking about bowling and write down what she would say. Tell your students to imagine that person, whose voice they know so well, talking about something they would enthusiastically speak about. By choosing a topic the person has a definite opinion about, emotion or particular attitude will naturally emerge. This exercise, like responding to the questionnaire, is one that students tend to do without much struggle, often beautifully capturing voice, rhythm, nuance, attitude (and thereby revealing lots about the character). It's yet another way to reassure young writers that they hold this particular element of good storytelling—capturing distinct voices—within them. When monologues are read aloud, ask the listeners to say what they learned about the character from his or her monologue. Ask the writers to underline their favorite lines, the ones they feel best capture the voice and spirit of the character. Many of the chosen lines would probably transfer well to dialogue exchanges.

➦ *Another Exercise for Dialogue:* Help your students focus on the dynamics of dialogue, the back-and-forth, the rhythms. Have them choose and examine a chunk of dialogue from a book they particularly like or examine a passage together as a class. Cut the passage down to pure dialogue (no tags or extra lines of description, gesture, etc.) Ask volunteers to read the dialogue as if in a play, speaking back and forth to one another to get a feel for the rhythm. Ask others to name the mood the exchange conveys, the information it imparts. Then go back to the original piece and have them identify what information other than actual dialogue was woven into the exchange—gesture, setting, detail.

All these exercises offer up chances to point out how the punctuation involved in written dialogue works, according to your students' level. It can be as minimal as identifying and naming quotation marks or as involved as indentation, placement of commas, what belongs inside and what belongs outside the quotation marks, and so forth. At any level, it's worth noting that all the little marks are there to help guide the reader. Punctuation is another tool the writer uses to make sure his or her story is read exactly as intended. Grammar and punctuation, contrary to some opinion, are not an endless bunch of rules that exist solely to torture and be tested on.

POINT OF VIEW

Related to character is the amazing, dizzying element of *point of view*. Point of view has everything to do with consciousness and goes hand in hand with the question, "Whose story is it?" Point of view is an aspect of narration, narrative voice, and narrative distance, among other ridiculously complex terms and notions. Here and now I am going to do my best to keep things simple.

The essential thing young writers need to grasp is that the person who is telling the story—the narrator—tells it from a certain point of view and from a certain amount of distance. The writer is in charge of choosing and establishing the point of view and the amount of distance. Much of that work happens naturally, often without the writer's awareness. Helping young writers become even slightly more conscious of narrative voice and narrative distance will give them a greater handle on their material and their choices for how to render it.

Aha

I attended Catholic schools growing up. One Easter, in a play about the Passion of Christ, I was given the role of one of the thieves crucified on either side of Jesus. Something the nun said made me realize that the thief—me—would have had a completely different understanding/experience than Jesus, whose point of view regarding the crucifixion was the only one I'd ever been given or thought about before that. It was an aha moment: realizing that people could have widely and wildly different points of view about the same experience. It was thrilling, as I remember. It opened a new world to me—thinking about and imagining how other people might feel about events that were happening, based on where they came from and how their lives had gone up to that point. I remember feeling that it was like taking a trip to do that imagining.

Role-playing—so basic and obvious—may be a good starting point for introducing your students to the basic premise of point of view. It's also a natural lead-in to a discussion of empathy. Have them take different roles and think about how the given character is thinking and feeling. To return to our touchstone, Peter Rabbit, ask them to consider how the story would change if Mr. McGregor told it!

When my kids were in school, they were both assigned exercises to write from a shoe's or a pencil's point of view. Such exercises miss entirely the wonder of point of view, which has everything to do with a new and different sensibility, emotional response, attitude. Why pick an inanimate object like a shoe? Sure, it's been done, sometimes even successfully. But I think it's a hard enough leap to make from one mind and heart to another without having to make the transfer to a shoe. Imagining the perspective of another person or an animal, perhaps, seems a much better way to invite a young writer to transfer thoughts and feelings, especially if that creature is caught in a particularly tense or interesting circumstance, one that is bound to elicit real emotional response.

In any case, remind your students that characters in a story all have their own versions of what is going on. Some versions get emphasized more than others, depending on how the story is written. The narrator has an especially strong say.

FIRST PERSON, THIRD PERSON, OMNISCIENT NARRATOR

Here are samples of narrative voices:

First-Person Narrator: *I don't like cake, never have. Not even on my birthday. Pizza's way better.*

Third-Person Narrator: *Anna didn't have much of a sweet tooth. At her tenth birthday party, she skipped the cake—a multilayer chocolate cake—in favor of more pizza.*

Omniscient Narrator: *On a warm June day, twelve girls gathered to celebrate the tenth birthday of Anna Rodriguez. Before the birthday cake was even brought out, Mary, the youngest of the group, sneaked into the kitchen, swiped her finger across the back of it, and helped herself to a gooey bite of frosting.*

Later, when it came time for Anna to cut the cake she noticed that someone had already sampled a bit. Anna didn't mind. She didn't care for cake, never had.

First, the basics. Someone tells the story, and that someone is the narrator. Most young writers (and many advanced ones as well) do not consciously choose to write their stories in first or third person, at least in the first draft. They simply start writing the story, and one voice or another emerges to tell it. I find young writers come to understand what the terms *first person*, *third person*, and *omniscient narrator* mean when they can see them in their own stories. So it never hurts to simply acknowledge what they have done in their stories: "I see you've chosen to write your story in third person—you refer to your main character as 'he.'" Or, "So, you're writing a story in first person—your main character is 'I.'" Or, "Your story has an omniscient narrator who knows everything that is going on and is watching many different characters." Sometimes that simple acknowledgment is enough, as far as you need to go. Sometimes it's appropriate to point out the advantages and limitations of the various kinds of narration.

First-person narration—"I" tells the story and is often the main character—is strictly limited to what that "I" can see and know. The narrator cannot go outside his or her limited perspective, into the minds and hearts of other characters. The voice of the narrator dominates, and it needs to be distinct and interesting. Of course, all the voices in a story need to be distinct and interesting, but with first-person narration the demand is even greater. Why choose a first-person narrator if his or her voice isn't going to come ringing off the page, consistent and compelling throughout the entire story? (If a student is adamant about staying with a first-person narration but the voice is dull, then it may be time to stop and concentrate on some of the isolated voice exercises suggested in Chapter 8.)

First-person narration allows the author to go deep inside the narrator's mind and heart, although simply using first-person narration doesn't guarantee that the author can or will take advantage of the opportunity. A common misperception among emerging writers is that writing in first person is easier and that it automatically ensures greater immediacy and intimacy. In my experience, practically nothing about writing is easy, and immediacy and intimacy have to be earned—and can be achieved—in a wide range of narrative voices. That said, many of your students will choose to write first-person autobiographical stories, and you can encourage them to make the most of it, to dig down deep to reveal thoughts, feelings, and insights about what is happening in the story and to settle into a clear and consistent voice.

Third-person narration limited to one particular character offers much the same potential for going deep inside a character. I used this kind of narration in *What Jamie Saw* (1995; see excerpt in Chapter 2, page 26) and felt that it allowed me to get as close to my character, Jamie, as I needed to be to tell the story I wanted to tell.

In third-person limited narration, the writer sticks with the main character at all times, never veering away and never losing track of him or her. Unlike first-person narration, however, the narrator has a voice separate from the main character and can also move a bit beyond and around the character. The narrator can slip in information and say things that don't have to come directly from the main character. With third-person limited narration, the narrator rides on the shoulder of the main character, occasionally dropping inside his heart, as opposed to first-person narration, in which the narrator, for better or worse, is trapped inside the character's brain, heart, and voice at all times.

An omniscient narrator knows everything, can travel everywhere, and can be with and inside a multitude of characters. An omniscient narrator is mighty. An omniscient narrator often gives a story a more distant, storytelling-of-old feel. You probably won't encounter it rising naturally from your young writers—as you will with first- and third-person narration—but, again, it's worth pointing out to them when you come across it in stories, to make them aware of yet another way of telling a story.

Exercises for Exploring Narration and Narrative Distance

Here are some exercises that play with degrees of separation—between the writer and his or her story and the narrator and the story.

◆ Have your students write a personal narrative about some meaningful incident in their lives. Then simply have them change the names of everyone in the story. Choosing names is fun, interesting, and revealing, and that one small act can make a difference, can activate and exercise a muscle of change in the writer and allow him or her to take a step away from the story and perhaps see it in a slightly different light.

◆ Another variation: Change the story from first-person narration into third-person narration and give the main character—the writer—a different name. That will make the biggest impression, create a distinction between author and character, and perhaps usher in the freedom and possibility inherent in fiction.

◆ A bigger variation: Have your students take that personal narrative and change the ending. Make it turn out differently, come to a different conclusion. Make a happy story sad or a sad story happy. Or give a resolved story a hanging ending. This variation does not change the narrative voice or point of view, but it allows young writers to exercise their power to alter and direct their stories.

➡ Read your students the opening pages of a book written in first–person narration and a book written in third-person narration and ask them what differences they notice. Have them write a paragraph or short scene in either first or third person and then switch what they have done, from first to third or from third to first. Refer to the simple sampling of narrators on page 115 in this chapter to introduce this exercise. When they have made the changes from "I" to "he" or "she," ask them to look for what other changes need to be made to make the scene satisfying. Ask them how the changed scene makes them feel, and if they like it better or not, and why.

These exercises will help your students start to know that they have choices when it comes to who will tell their stories, from what point of view, and from what amount of distance. These are tricky concepts to talk about and wrap one's head around, but young writers of any age can be introduced to them.

Chapter 10

PLACE AND TIME

$\mathcal{E}$very story takes place *somewhere*. Every story unfolds over some period of time. Setting and time frame are story elements that can play an important role in how a story is told and whether it is successful. Choices regarding setting and time intersect with all the other elements and affect the entire story.

PLACE

Some writers are particularly attentive to setting—attuned to nature, deeply rooted in a certain area, or comfortable describing a highly imagined otherworld—and focusing on this aspect of story writing will allow them to dip into their stash of details and observations about certain places. For others who have a less-developed sense of place or less curiosity about how characters interact with their environment, paying focused attention to setting can awaken them to a new dimension.

The key thing, early on, is to help young writers simply become conscious of *where* a story or scene unfolds. Once they are aware of that element they can turn their attention to description, focusing on particular details and nuances of that place, and begin to discover how that place might factor in contributing to the mood of the story.

Setting offers you another element to address and zoom in on in responding to your students' stories, asking for more or less description, perhaps greater grounding. Remind your young writers that readers need to know where a story is happening and want to have a genuine feel for the place.

Stories can unfold in one or many settings. Let's keep it simple and return to our old friend Peter Rabbit to consider the places where his story unfolds. As with many classic tales, his story starts and ends at home. Home is where the heart is, and in his case where his mother, sisters, safety, and chamomile tea are, too. In some stories, home is the scene of the crime. For many characters, it's the place they long to return to, and for others it's the place they can't wait to leave. Almost any time home (or the absence of home) appears in a story, it carries a great deal of emotional clout.

Home is the setting that bookends the beginning and ending of Peter's story. Through text and pictures, the reader gets a sense of the place where Peter lives, the environs of his home "underneath the root of a very big fir-tree." The middle of the story, though, plays out entirely on forbidden territory, in various settings on Mr. McGregor's property: all over his garden, from the beans and parsley to the cabbages and gooseberries; in the toolshed; at the wall; by the pond; and at the gate. Although it's not a vast area of land, each new setting contributes to each plot development, and each place is distinct and different from the others.

When a setting changes, it usually signals a new paragraph or scene of the story. A change in setting indicates that a story is moving on, literally, to another place as well as to another development and perhaps to a different emotional tone.

Starting Close to Home

Everyone holds places within their memories and hearts and minds. Everyone comes from somewhere, lives somewhere, has visited or dreamed of other places near or far.

As with much they are familiar with, familiar settings are often dismissed by young writers as unexciting or uninteresting. Many students feel they must go to some version of outer space to be anywhere interesting. Outer space may indeed be interesting, but they'll need to describe, understand, and know it as well as they know their own backyards, and so their own backyards are often a good place to start. Again, it's another opportunity to encourage them to value and know that which surrounds them and to take advantage of something they already know about.

In my early novels, I consciously chose to set my stories in places (houses, neighborhoods, towns, cities, areas of the country) in which I had lived or knew well. I was struggling with so many other parts of the story—character, plot, structure—that it came as a relief to write with authority about a known location. It was one way to make writing a short story or novel, which often felt overwhelming and intimidating, seem more manageable. I also found that familiar settings held deep reservoirs of emotional connections.

TIME

Time is an element—and has a role to play—in every story. As delicious and fun as playing around with time can be, at least in our imagination, handling time in a story is usually tricky and can feel terribly awkward at first. There are a number of ways to talk about time and to approach it with your students.

Time Frame

Time frame is another one of those touchstones I return to again and again, as both writer of and responder to stories. I love the literal clarity of the term, time *frame*—a frame in which the whole story plays out.

One of the most helpful responses I ever received from my editor about a story was, "What if this story happened over a weekend instead of a week?" Answering that one simple question gave me a way to rethink and simplify the entire story I'd written. The suggestion—a practical and concrete lesson about the uses of time frame—was also a positive way to respond to a story that was too long and pokey. Shortening the time frame forced me to condense and tighten the scenes, to figure out what really needed to be there and what did not. My editor identified the problem (slow pacing, text longer than needed) by asking a question. He did not presume to tell me exactly how to solve the problem; he simply invited me to envision my story in a tighter time frame, and he trusted me to do the work of revising accordingly. The more we respect our young writers, the more they will come along without feeling that we have taken their stories away from them.

An important question we can ask of any writer about any story is, "Over how long a time period does your story take place?"

It's a clear and simple question, and the answer will sometimes help the writer see his or her story in a different way, from a different perspective.

Some stories end up breaking down into natural units of time: minutes, hours, days, nights, weeks, months. Once the writer has that awareness, he or she can figure out what and how much happens in each segment of the overall time. Sometimes, in an early draft of a story, I'll end up spending many pages on a scene that takes place in several minutes or hours and then have scenes that gallop through much longer periods of time, which often creates a jerky feeling to the story. There are no hard-and-fast rules about how time is doled out and accounted for (or about anything else), but the writer needs to be conscious of the passage of time in any given scene and aware that every part of every story is grounded in past, present, or future. Once they become aware, they can make conscious choices about how much of the story to devote to a certain chunk of time and consider whether, overall, they have achieved the flow and pacing that's right for their story.

Past and Present: Tenses

When a story takes place is a basic choice that the writer makes and needs to be aware of. Did the story take place recently, a while ago, or hundreds of years ago? Regardless of when the story actually took place, does the writer want the narrator to present it as though it were happening right now? Just as many writers choose first- or third-person narration without giving it much thought, many writers choose the tense in which they write their stories—past or present—without much consideration. The story simply "comes out" in past tense or in present tense. That unconscious choice tells us something—if only that we feel most comfortable or familiar with that tense. Early on, familiarity may be a good enough reason to stick with it. However, it's never too early to make the author aware of what he or she has done: to name the tense in which the draft is written, to clarify that a story written in past tense is being told as something that has already happened. A story told in present tense reads as if it is unfolding in the moment. There is no chance for retrospective musing or comments. Some writers choose to use present tense to make the story feel more immediate. Have your writers think about when the story they are writing happened and have them consider from what distance—how far back—the narrator is remembering it.

Some young writers struggle with shifting tenses—they swing from past to present to past again—maybe because they are still getting comfortable with using consistent tenses or maybe because they haven't entirely settled on when the story takes place. Pointing out the tense slippage *in terms of time* may be more helpful to the writer than simply registering it as a grammatical correction. As writers make the necessary changes, they will settle into a story grounded in a particular time that is less likely to confuse the reader.

Flashbacks and Backstory

Some simple stories unfold chronologically in a chosen time, incorporating very little background information or memories. Most stories, however, blend in background, historical information, and memories as they go along. There is a main story that unfolds, and there may be longer and shorter references to a time *before* that. Many beginning writers of all ages stumble trying to incorporate material from the past into whatever is happening in the forward-moving story. Shifting in and out of the main narrative calls for a particular and exercised set of writing muscles. (This aspect of story

writing may be more advanced than
some of your writers need to address. If
so, skip this section, or return to it
when you have a student who is
clearly grappling with it.)

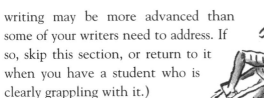

When I was working
on my first novel, *Tell Me
Everything* (1993), incorporating flashbacks was the
single most difficult
technical challenge I
faced. The ongoing
story involved Roz's journey to find out
how exactly her mother had died, but that
journey was predicated on and evoked many
memories of earlier life with her mother in the
North Country of New Hampshire. I struggled to
keep the story moving forward even as I needed to
take occasional steps back into Roz's past with her
mother. How to weave them in? How to
strike the balance?

Background, backstory, context, and *flashbacks* all describe the
kind of information from the past that I am talking about. Once
again, none of these terms mean much to young writers until they
are struggling to incorporate material into stories of their own.
Then, helping them to see what it is they are trying to do—isolating
and addressing the challenge—is the first step. Sometimes the background information is simple, clear, and factual. Sometimes it
involves a poignant memory with emotional resonance, revealed
though a little story all its own.

Some writers are naturally able and inclined to drop in necessary background information as they go along, offering clarification
about dates, places, where someone came from, or what work they
do. These are the concrete details and bits of information that can
be simply stated and which help broaden a story. My rule of thumb
for this kind of information is simply to put it in as needed, as
quickly and clearly as possible: *My father worked at the factory in
Monroeville.* Or, *When I was six years old I lived in Fort Wayne,
Indiana, with my grandmother, Emma Madella Jackson.* Sentences like
that, which provide specific facts about place and background, go a
long way in grounding the reader. They sometimes call for changes
in tense from the ongoing story but mostly just slip naturally into the
ongoing narrative. The other rule of thumb regarding this kind of
background information is to say only as much as is needed and to
be as specific as possible.

Our friend Mrs. Rabbit provides a lovely example of inserting
crucial background information into the story, quickly and economically: "Your father was put in a pie."

Flashbacks are longer and trickier to weave into a story. They
involve a step back in both time and memory. They are remembered
events or moments that happened before the unfolding events in the
main story. The essential question that must be addressed is why the
flashback needs and deserves to be where it is at that exact point in
the story.

Flashbacks often assert themselves naturally—the writer will be
writing about one thing in the unfolding narrative and suddenly be
reminded of something that happened earlier that somehow ties in.
Such connections can deepen a story, and the challenge is to insert
the flashback smoothly and seamlessly without losing the thread of
the ongoing narrative. How do you let the reader know that the

story is taking a step back in time? Many young writers draw undue attention to entering the memory by having their characters "gaze" off into the distance and "think back to the day when. . . ." Better to take a firm and quick step back, right into the memory. For those who are grammatically challenged, how do you make all those changes from present tense to past tense or from past tense to past perfect? The awkwardness of going from *has* to *had* and from *had* to *had had*! Do you have to put a *had* in front of every verb for the entire flashback? (No, you don't. You only have to make sure that readers understand where they are in the story.)

Entry and departure, placement, emotional tone, and impact are the main considerations writers need to keep in mind when dealing with flashbacks. They need to be entered and exited simply and clearly. They need to be placed in just the right spot. They should not go on and on and on. They need to have emotional resonance with what's happening in the main story. There needs to be a connection or association, however tenuous, that adds to or deepens the overall story. They need to be thoughtfully spaced so that they don't end up hijacking the unfolding story.

Here's a flashback from my novel *Many Stones* (2000). Berry and her father are in South Africa to attend a memorial service for Berry's sister, Laura, who was murdered there. Her father has just announced to Berry that he has scheduled a tour of Soweto.

> *"And no," he says. "I am not kidding about the tour." He is loosening his necktie and unbuttoning the top button of his shirt.*
>
> *"Fine," I say and go into my bedroom and close the door.*
>
> *I kneel down and reach for my shoes under the bed and remember the first Christmas Laura came home from college after Mom and Dad had split up. Dad and I picked Laura up at*

the airport and then Dad took us out to dinner at the Press Club in Washington, his favorite place. I was so sad when Laura automatically climbed in the front next to him and they right away got into some big discussion about whether Americans should invest in South African companies. I watched the back of Laura's head—she'd gotten her hair cut and her neck looked so different to me—and her profile when she turned to him: "Dad, it's morally indefensible."

I could feel how much Dad loved discussing politics with Laura, even though they were arguing, and it was so clear to me that Laura had gone over and been welcomed into territory I didn't know anything about. I felt a thousand miles down the road from where they were, up front with the steering wheel and all the lights and controls on the panel of the dashboard.

That night Laura sat with me in back on the way home, French-braided my hair, asked about my friends at school. Dad referred to himself as James, the chauffeur, but I knew there was no catching up.

And I know there's no not going to Soweto. (51–53)

The focus of the story shifts from the unfolding narrative (Berry and her father in South Africa) to Berry's memory of being with her father and sister and feeling excluded. She remembers a specific evening and place and how she felt. Her emotional response is at the core of her memory. She did not feel like she fit in; she did not know or care about what so interested her father and sister. A simple connecting thought brings her back to the present moment: she cannot get out of the dreaded tour anymore than she felt she could catch up with her father and sister and their grown-up concerns and discussion. The tenses alternate from present tense to past and back to present. The flashback underscores her feelings of not being part of what's going on. Having no say in what they are doing underscores the painful absence of Laura. It's a relatively short and quick memory, and then the main story clicks in again.

Often flashbacks end up being little stories unto themselves, and they need to be pared down to whatever essence connects them to and belongs with the larger story. Frequently, writers instinctively and unconsciously choose a flashback for all the right reasons. Then they need to figure out what's at its core, why it belongs where it does, and boil it down to its emotional essence. Sometimes they need help in figuring out that essence—help in the form of questions and more questions.

I spend hours and hours working on flashbacks to get them in the right place, to shape and polish them to resonate with the larger story, to flow as seamlessly as possible into and out of them. Doing that work often helps me to understand what the larger story is all about, too. Flashbacks often hold clues.

Exercises That Focus on Place and Time and Flashbacks

•➔ Ask your students to choose a place they love—from having lived or visited there or from having imagined it thoroughly. Ask them to tell you about that place in detail. What does it look like and smell like? What is the weather there? What are the colors? Now ask them to choose a place they don't like, don't want to ever see again, and ask them to tell you about that place. Compare the words and phrases of the two descriptions. Talk about which one is strongest, and figure out why that is. Is it word choice? Background information? Details?

- It doesn't take long to make a connection between place and emotion. I've often given this exercise, borrowed from John Gardner's *The Art of Fiction* (1984), to my students. "Describe a landscape as seen by an old woman whose disgusting and detestable husband has just died. Do not mention the husband or the death." You can adapt the prompt to fit your class, your age group, the writer you are working with in a one-on-one conference. You can revise it so that the unspoken emotion is funny, light, or confused. It doesn't have to be death that makes the point that how we feel affects how we see. This exercise, as well as prompting a description of place or setting, also addresses the tricky notion of emotional tone, which is crucial in storytelling.

- Maps and models are other ways you might invite your students to show the places they are interested in, that hold meaning for them. Basically, you are looking for ways to bring forth, isolate, and concentrate on this aspect of *where*, because where something happens makes a difference and has a role to play in telling a story.

- Invite your students to think about different blocks of time that have meaning to them: school week, semester, summer vacation, special birthday years, favorite seasons, and so on. Talk about how each of those blocks of times can serve as a frame for a story—

the time within which the story unfolds. Certain periods can be particularly rich in memories and sensory associations and can therefore offer up possible material for a story. They also set limits for how much time the author has to deal with—an entire life, a single afternoon, the year the author turned thirteen, or a particular holiday weekend where everything changed.

➻ Have your young writers find a flashback in the book they are currently reading. That act alone—identifying it—is the start of understanding a flashback and how it works. Then have the writer underline the line or phrase that ushers the reader away from the unfolding story and into the memory. Have the writer underline the phrase or sentences that usher the reader out of the flashback and back into the story. Have the reader say in a sentence or two what the flashback is about. What is the emotional essence of the flashback? In what way does it connect to what is going on in the unfolding story?

This last exercise can be used to introduce your students to writing flashbacks, but I think it'll be more effective if it's saved until someone is actually trying to write one and finding out how difficult it is. To this day, I still am most helped by critical analysis when it addresses a problem I'm up against in my own writing.

COMBINING THE ELEMENTS

*H*aving deconstructed the story into its component elements, it's now time to bring them all together and write a story, beginning to end. A first draft comes first. Then comes revision (one more draft at the very least or if you're like me or any of the writers I know, dozens), and then comes a final copyedit and proofreading. How you allot time for these stages is yours to juggle, but each part is important, and the sooner your students come to know and engage with all the steps along the way, the further along they'll be as writers.

DRAFTS

Some writers are fearless when it comes to creating the first draft. They have energy, enthusiasm, and the ability to let the ideas and words pour out. The blank page is an invitation, not a threat. For others, getting the first draft down is torture. Maybe they'll always feel that way, or maybe they'll have a different experience with each story they write. In any case, writing a first draft is challenging and challenges each writer in his or her particular way. There are technical and craft demands; vulnerability and fear of failure; different levels of interest, attention, and talent; emotional connections to whatever material they are dealing with; resistance to the unknown and to hard work.

If you, the teacher, are not writing stories yourself, you will have a hard time appreciating how difficult it can be for your students, and you may not be as supportive or responsive as you need to be.

Keep asking about the stories your students have to tell. Keep encouraging and reminding them that good stories take time and practice to write. Tell students who worry excessively about making every word and sentence perfect that they don't need to get everything right the first time around.

Once students are working on first drafts of a story, that's all they can do: work on them, build them word by word, sentence by sentence, scene by scene, in their own ways, at their own pace. (I assume there will be one-on-one conferences during this stage, and I address ways to respond to stories-in-progress in Chapter 14.) As far as where the writers are, they are in their drafts. They need the time, the place, and repeated sessions to do their work. Of course, you are on hand to help and encourage, but essentially they must reach inside themselves and their material in order to get that first draft out and down on paper. Encourage, prod, push, cajole if necessary, but get them to finish a complete draft, because then they have something to work with. A first draft is a gold mine.

Revision

Revision is an essential part of creating a story and a process unto itself that needs acknowledgment, encouragement, and guidance. With many beginning writers, revision is a hard sell. Asking someone to go back to work on something he or she has already worked on—something he or she may already think is perfect or which he or she may be sick to death of—is a lot to ask.

A few things your young writers need to know: revision is essential. No one gets it exactly right the first (or second or third) time around. Often, when I go into classrooms to talk to young writers, I bring the mountain of papers that constitute the drafts of a story I have written—hundreds and hundreds of pages to get to the final (skinny) story! I also mention that it usually takes me two to three *years* to write a book!

For students to be willing to tackle the hard work of revision, they need to care about the material in the first place. If they care about it, they will want to get it right, and revision is their chance. Remind them that their drafts are rich and filled with clues they can now identify and follow. They need reasons to plow through this part of the process, and once they begin the work they need encouragement to keep at it.

Help your writers decide what to tackle in revision. (I address many approaches to responding to stories in Chapters 12—15.) Choose a doable amount. Let them know that a final proofreading will catch any remaining spelling and grammar changes. Allow them to learn what revision really is: literally, seeing again, seeing more. This is the chance to clarify and enlarge their stories and to emphasize the parts that speak to what the story is really about.

Give them time, a quiet place, encouragement. Tend to the ones who seem especially stuck.

COPYEDITING AND PROOFREADING

Sometimes when I go into classrooms, I bring along the manuscript that my editor has marked up, and the one the proofreader has marked up after that, catching all the misplaced commas and out-of-control semicolons and misspellings. I love telling kids that I am only a mediocre speller and that I punctuate more according to instinct than to rules I learned in school but have forgotten. I know I may be saying things that some teachers don't want to hear—teachers who need, want, and must deliver when it comes to spelling mastery, punctuation skills, and proficiency. I am not making light of these demands you face, not at all. I'm just saying it can be a comfort to a child to hear that a good story can be written without perfect spelling and grammar in the first (or early) draft(s). Different parts of my stories are tended to along the way; not everything comes together all at once. Why should we ask kids to do what professional writers don't even have to do? The first challenge for me is to find a story to write about, to gather some crumbs—a plot incident or a character I'm interested in. Later, I fine-tune the writing, reorder passages, and, with help from my editor, copyeditor, and proofreader, incorporate all the changes that make it complete.

I've worked with young writers who resisted writing a story out of fear of misspelling words, students who equated good writing only with good spelling. They must be helped to expand their understanding of what constitutes a good story.

Making sure that there is a final proofreading of the story for correct grammar and punctuation (appropriate to your students' level) ensures that you are addressing this aspect and allows the focus to be on the content and crafting of the story early on. Fair enough?

Things Worth Waiting for in Writing a Story

Writing a good story takes time. Much of that time the writer may feel that things aren't going well. Over the years, I've experienced the ebb and flow of hope and discouragement in my own writing life. I still struggle with worries, doubts, exhaustion, and discouragement, but I know that they are part of my process. I also know that there are things worth waiting for—parts of the story that seem to come in their own, sweet (and sometimes not-so-sweet) time: getting to know my characters, for instance. Their names. Their voices. A plot that is believable and organic. Connections within the story. Knowing what it's about at its core. Things come when they come, one at a time, usually; never all at once or all together. So sometimes, it's good to gratefully acknowledge what your young writer has already accomplished. Both writer and teacher need to remember that stories are written bit by bit, over time, and with help.

Reading Work Aloud

Sometimes reading a draft aloud and receiving feedback from fellow writers can offer the author valuable insight into how to approach revision. Much depends on the listeners' skill in responding and whether they can articulate what impressed them and what they didn't understand or wanted to know more about. A truly responsive and helpful group of fellow writers is formed over time and as each member develops individually. (I say more about listening and responding to stories in Chapter 15.)

At any stage, reading aloud is a brave act on the part of the writer and deserves acknowledgment. The author may be caught up in the reading and unable to listen intently to the feedback; it's our job as teachers to remind the writer, when he or she *can* hear, of key remarks and questions. Protect young writers from bombardment or runaway discussions of their stories. Make sure they take away a few specific responses and suggestions that can guide them in their revision.

If nothing else, readings usually provide a good basic gauge of interest level. When someone reads a strong story—one that makes the listeners pay attention and feel something in response to what they've heard—a palpable current goes through the group. Listeners become animated, and there is spontaneous feedback and questions. The writer blossoms and glows and is encouraged to continue.

EXERCISES DURING REVISION

Here are a few exercises to try sometime during the revision process. They cannot be done until there is some kind of finished draft in hand that the writer is attempting to shape and polish.

- Making a storyboard of what they've got so far in their drafts can sometimes be helpful—a way to spot redundancies or missing pieces. The distillation of plot and a character's emotional journey might at least offer clues about which part of the story requires the most attention.

- Sometimes it can help to ask the writer to clearly and concisely say what a story is about—for example, in the form of flap copy or story summary. It sounds simple enough, but it's not. (I often don't know what my stories are about until I've written many drafts or until my writers' group or my editor tells me.)

So try this exercise. Have your students make a cover for their story and write the so-called flap copy for it: the concise paragraph that tells readers what the story is about. It's a demanding exercise—a killer, actually—because it forces the writer to concisely and clearly summarize what happens to whom over what time period, as well as the tone of the story (funny, serious, emotional, rip-roaring) and what it all addresses. This exercise forces the author to speak well of his or her work. You will never read flap copy that apologizes for or denigrates the story it describes.

When I have tried this exercise for my own books-in-progress, it has often pointed out to me where I am in trouble: beginning, middle, or end. Obviously, one cannot say everything that happens in a book—the writer must choose what's most important or interesting to mention. The author may also discover that he or she is vague when it comes to articulating what happens in certain parts of the story. It can be a quick way to identify the most obvious weak link. As revision progresses, so too will the flap copy. It will go from vague and flabby to clean and trim.

The story summary is a variation on this theme. It can be a little longer and doesn't have to have the upbeat energy of flap copy. But, again, it forces the writer to pare down the draft to its essential actions and characters. It's another attempt to manage the material and say what it's about, without judgment. It's not saying what isn't there but simply what is.

➳ You might also ask students to create flap copy or story summaries for other students' stories—to develop their ability to condense and articulate what they have read and to give the author a sense of what he or she has communicated.

Part Three

RESPONDING TO STORIES,
SUPPORTING REVISION

Chapter 12

TOUCHSTONES

$\mathcal{T}$here are as many ways to respond to stories as there are stories—both stories-in-progress and final drafts. Responding to someone face to face, having just read or listened to his or her story, is different from reading a writer's work in private, with time to consider and formulate a written response. Responding to a rough draft is different from responding to a finished story. Each instance calls on different critical faculties.

Most of our responses are made to stories-in-progress, in support of the revision process. I hold on to a few fundamentals when I am critiquing drafts, just as there are touchstones I have when I am writing.

One of the best pieces of advice I was ever given from a colleague was to think of the *single* most important response that could be made to any given story. We hear or read a story and may have lots of reactions; many things may come to mind regarding how and why it does or doesn't succeed. But what's the one thing that matters most, that gets to the heart of the story and the writer's intention, the one thing that might make the biggest difference in improving the piece, from all the possible points of improvement? To articulate that single thing requires looking into the story, past the obvious small corrections that need to be made, in search of the fundamental knot that keeps the story from realizing its intention. The ability to identify the key issue demands that we truly understand stories ourselves. The problem may be structural; it may have to do with character development, runaway plot, or affectless voice. Our job is to identify the core issue or confusion—to name it, and to ask for clarification—all at a level appropriate to the story and the writer. Settling on the basic question or comment about a story is our chance, as teachers, to practice what we preach: pare down, hone, and respectfully address what we see as the heart of the matter. That one response is sometimes the only one called for, the only one worth saying. Other times it can be the springboard for a wide-ranging consideration of the story.

Ask Genuine Questions

Asking clear and genuine questions is another touchstone I rely on in responding to stories. I ask questions every time I consider my own drafts and every time I read the stories of others. *What do you mean? Why is this here? How does this part connect to what came before it? How does your character feel when this is happening?* There are a million and one honest, simple questions to be asked—without attitude, frustration, or judgment—to help the writer write the clearest, best story he or she can. Please note: asking the question doesn't mean the writer knows (should know or can know) the answer yet.

Questions are seeds, and the best ones take root, get the writer thinking and wondering about new possibilities. We're just asking. If the answer isn't clear, then the story is still evolving. The writer needs to write more to discover the answers.

Coming up with the right questions requires seeing into the draft before us: what is there, and, sometimes, more important, what isn't there yet. We respond by picking up on the clues inherent in the draft: spots that have the most juice or electricity; parts that jump the rails of what the story seemed to be about; insights into character that bear further emphasis and refining; flashes of underlying emotion, humor, or sadness; burning questions buried beneath an avalanche of action. Drafts are a gold mine of clues about where the story wants and needs to go next, and our job as teachers is to see those clues, articulate them, and urge the writer to follow them.

Truly, the best questions are the ones you really want to know the answer to, and so they will naturally emerge and be specific to the story you are reading. But here are a few open-ended questions that I've found often elicit surprising answers and helpful clues about possible ways to proceed:

Where did this story come from?
Is there something you know that you're not telling in this
    story?
What part do *you* like the best? Why?
Are there parts of the story that kind of drag you down and
    make you want to quit writing it?
What things do you know for sure belong in this story?

Add questions of your own to this list, ones that prime the pump of your conversation about a story-in-progress.

Choose and Concentrate on Specific Story Elements

The story elements that we concentrated on in constructing a story also come into play in responding to one. The narrative arc that guides me in writing also guides me in responding—reminds me that I can consider the story in terms of its beginning, middle, end; its rising tension, climax, and resolution; its overall shape. It's reassuring that a story can be broken down to various parts and elements and can be responded to in that way. Concentrating on identified aspects of a story removes the pressure to tackle everything at once. Doing so divides the problem and makes what can seem overwhelming in its totality (a complete short story, a novel, a term paper, a complete anything!) seem doable; it breaks it down into manageable, identifiable parts.

Isolate and consider various elements. Identify the time frame. Look exclusively at the dialogue, or focus on the key actions of the story. Taking one thing at a time prevents a mishmash of responses that can overwhelm the writer. You have a choice in what you respond to and when!

Address Level of Interest

Addressing the level of interest is another gauge in responding to any story. (Sometimes, honestly, the question is, Is there *anything* of interest in this story?) And what is the writer's level of engagement with his or her story?

If a story is not interesting to its author, what are the chances that anyone else will be interested? A writer's interest in his or her topic does not guarantee that the piece will engage others, but a writer who's *not* interested in the material pretty much guarantees that no one else will be either. Whatever the topic, fiction or nonfiction, there has to be a point of connection between the writer and what is written. Sometimes that point of connection only becomes evident after the story is written. Other times writers know the point of connection going in. Either way, it's got to be there. Invite the writer to think about it. What really interests them the most in what they are writing about? What is it they truly want to convey? Sometimes it's an idea or moral. Sometimes it's a mood— they want what they write to be scary, sad, or a big surprise. Sometimes it's to reveal something they feel strongly about, a shout-out from their hearts to others. There are many good reasons to write all sorts of stories, and our job is to help our students discover their material and intentions. Responding to a draft or a story in these terms lets them know that we care about receiving stories that matter to them.

Tics

I use the word *tics* to describe certain writing habits that recur in a young writer's work. The tic can be a repeating grammatical error, a tendency to structure sentences in a certain way, a reliance on adjectives, a default to romantic-sounding language—a thousand different things. When you read carefully, you'll begin to see these recurring writing habits. Point them out so the writer can begin to see them, too. It's not a judgment call or a criticism. It's merely a habit you've noticed that needs to be brought to a conscious level for the writer. It's a piece of information you can share as both the writer and the story emerge.

The Story You See

My editor taught me a way to respond to material that I fall back on time and time again. In his written response to the manuscript I send him, he always starts off by summarizing the story that he has read—to see if that's the story I meant to tell. It's such a simple and respectful act: saying back what you have read. So often, in reading his summary, I am able to see the parts of the story that were clear to me in my head and heart that did not come across in my draft. Starting to see the gap between what I intended and what I conveyed gives me a clear sense of what I need to address in revision.

I rely on this practice of saying back to the writer the story I have read, particularly when I am responding in writing but also in one-on-one conferences when I respond to scenes and sections of a story-in-progress. Brief summaries give the writer a sense of what he or she is or isn't communicating. Composing these responses also models a skill we want to encourage: the ability to distill and articulate stories, scenes, or moments with clarity and concision.

Setting the Bar

Finally, always be on the lookout for a part of the story that works beautifully—an exchange of dialogue, a particular scene, a thoroughly satisfying plot development. Identify it, praise it, and challenge the writer to bring the rest of the story up to that level. The writer has already shown that he or she is capable of such work. By setting the bar with something the writer has already accomplished, you both recognize the accomplishment and encourage revision of weaker sections.

Chapter 13

Drafts: Responding to Different Kinds of Stories and Story Parts

I n both writing and responding to a story, I look for ways to make things manageable, and that often involves concentrating on isolated elements or sections. A focused look at what kind of story it is, or at certain component parts, inevitably addresses other concerns, because the various parts of a story interconnect and work together.

I usually find it worthwhile to ask what kind of story it is or what kind of story it wants to be. Is it character driven or action based?

If someone writes about an experience, either made up or from real life, and it is filled with (or has the potential for) a lot of emotion, then mining the story for its emotional content is often the most important work for that writer to address in revision. Tracking the emotional journey of the main character might be a clear-cut way for the writer to see how the story needs to proceed in stages. Once again, basic questions emerge: What state is the main character in at the beginning of the story? How does he or she change? How is he or she feeling at any given point in the story? What state is the main character in at the end? What is the character doing and feeling in each scene, and do the scenes connect to one another? Has the writer been able to *show* how a character is feeling rather than simply naming or telling an emotion? In limiting your focus to the main character's emotional progression, you may be able to help the writer see and clarify the trajectory of the story.

I've had so many wonderful conversations with writers about their characters and what happened to them; the conversation becomes intimate as we discuss people we both know and care about, try to figure out an underlying motivation, move a step beyond what we started with, which is the draft. There are not right and wrong questions, only the ones that burrow inside what has already been written. Ask things you really want to know, say what interests you most, and listen up for that breakthrough line or explanation—the one to which you can respond, "Oh, *that's* what your character really wants!"

In an evolving, action-packed story, I turn my attention to the actions the writer has already chosen and consider whether they make sense and whether they escalate the tension properly to achieve the desired effect. I try to figure out what role the characters caught up in all the action play, and I look for basic character traits that emerge from scene to scene. The emphasis in responding is often on how the main actions can be refined and intensified.

The story must be interesting and cannot be devoid of emotional content or characterization, but the characters can be broad and somewhat more one dimensional. The character usually has one dominant trait that needs to be shown repeatedly as he or she generates or responds to what is happening in the story. Revision frequently involves paring things down, choosing the best incidents/adventures from the multitude often offered in a first draft.

Even stories that are clearly based on a popular video game or recently viewed movie are revealing of the writer. First, the writer has chosen *that* particular story to imitate. Something about it made a deep enough impression on him that he chose to recapitulate it. Sometimes figuring out the core of what interested him about it provides an insight into the child and that, on its own, is a gift.

BEGINNINGS, MIDDLES, AND ENDINGS

Sometimes responding specifically to the beginning, middle, or ending of a story can offer the writer a focused approach for revision; to make even one section of the story stronger is a challenge, and doing so constitutes real progress.

Beginnings

I like to think of beginnings as invitations. I've also heard the opening of a story referred to as a promise of what is to come.

Has your student started his or her story in the best possible place? Often the real start—the best line, the one with punch and interest is buried somewhere in the first paragraph, page, or scene of a draft. Be on the lookout for it if you sense a slow-going start. Sometimes, when the story is read aloud, you discover the true beginning of the story by registering the palpable rise in interest among listeners who had previously not been engaged.

Getting the beginning of a story just right is tough and often doesn't happen until the writer has figured out the ending. I work a long time on my beginnings, looking for a chosen moment or incident that somehow speaks to the larger concerns of the story and settling on the right tone.

An added challenge of beginnings is the need to figure out what must be told from the past for the current story to make sense. How much backstory to weave in as the story is taking off? That's tricky business. Sometimes it's helpful to list essential background information and then look for appropriate places in the opening pages where it can be inserted quickly and economically.

In responding to beginnings, you can ask yourself—and the author—whether it has laid the groundwork on which the entire story can unfold. Has it made a promise to the reader about what is going to come? Has it introduced the main character and set the action in play?

Just jump in; cut to the chase. These are two comments that I've written repeatedly in the course of responding to beginnings of all kinds—stories, chapters, scenes. Just get into the moment that has juice. Yes, readers need enough information and background so they won't be confused, but what readers really want is what's interesting: the dirt, the heart of the matter, the excitement, the chosen moment.

Middles

Middles are where things get complicated. Middles are where tension builds. Middles are where (more) things need to happen. Middles are where the plot thickens, or, as we say around my house, the plot sickens. Given how difficult it is for me to make many things happen, middles tend to be hard for me. The main questions I end up asking writers (including myself) about the middle of stories are, What happens next and why? What *could* happen next? What *needs* to happen next? What needs to happen in what order?

Sometimes the middle of a story suffers from not *enough* happening to create rising tension or complication. When stuck, when in doubt, we plot-challenged writers can always be directed back to the most basic plot-generating question: *What if?*

For young writers whose plot developments know no end or who are inclined to tell every single thing that happens, the middle is the place that can get most muddled. The remedy is to ask your young writers to identify and choose the most important actions, the ones that allow their characters to shine, that have real emotional content as well as action that escalates the tension.

With draft in hand (and often a draft that the young writer is completely satisfied with and believes cannot be improved), make a simple list of the story's main plot developments. Use a few key words or phrases to identify them. Then have the writer number the most important events. Sometimes this exercise of listing and prioritizing will make it quite clear that some scenes are redundant—that they basically hold the story still rather than moving it forward. In early drafts, I often unknowingly include two versions of the same (essential) scene. My job in revision is to choose the stronger one. Our job as teachers is to help young writers become aware of their choices.

The sequencing of the scenes also plays an important role in creating tension. Storyboarding their draft can offer them an overview of what they've got and a way to consider shuffling scenes around to affect the pacing and the tension.

In considering middles, be on the lookout for scenes or events that aren't linked together in a way that makes sense, irrelevant material, action completely devoid of emotional content, and no forward movement to the story. Work with your writers to identify which scenes work and which don't, and suggest the big, brave act of cutting whatever doesn't help the overall story. The ability to do that—cut material—is an essential muscle for young writers to develop.

Endings

My fiction editor often distinguishes between stories that end and stories that simply stop. You know the ones that just stop. You're reading along and suddenly you reach the last sentence. You're inclined to look for the next one, because something in you has been left unsatisfied. Stories, even ones with hanging or ambiguous endings, should leave the reader with a sense of completion. Has the story delivered on its promised journey? Does it end up somewhere new and different? Has something changed? An ending can be evaluated in all sorts of ways. When I am unsatisfied with an ending, I ask, *Is this* really *the end? Is there something you know that you're not telling me? Why did you decide to end it here? How do you want your reader to feel?* Sometimes responding with wishes is the way to go: *Oh, I wish you would tell me more. I wish I knew more about how the character felt. I wish it wasn't over yet.* Sometimes all a writer needs is to be asked.

An ending that goes beyond the *real* ending is also common (a variation on real beginnings that occur after the story has already started). I once hiked a mountain on a foggy day with a friend. We reached a spot close to what we thought was the summit and met a few other hikers already there, including a ranger. We exchanged hellos and then kept going, trailed by the ranger who finally called out to us, "Did you know that was the summit?" Well, no, we hadn't known, and we would have realized it on our own eventually, but the ranger helped us see it sooner. That's what readers/teachers/mentors/editors often do: help the writer see that they've already reached the summit, made the point, ended the story. Writing exacts so much concentration about so many things that often the writer cannot see what he or she has already done.

Many emerging writers consistently write past the line that should end the paragraph, the scene, the chapter, or the book. This often happens because writers do not trust that they have communicated what they meant to, and so they keep going, adding that extra line or paragraph. It's a tic that goes away with time, practice, and evolving trust in themselves and in their readers. In the meantime, they have teachers to help them see, and so that is our work: to see the ending, to open ourselves to being satisfied.

Responding to Building Blocks

Stories are made of words, sentences, paragraphs, and scenes, and each building block offers another aspect of story to respond to.

Words

Each word of a story is chosen. Which ones are extraneous, and which are especially delightful? Is there a single word you can praise as perfect? Once you've identified that word, some of the others around it may seem a little lackluster by comparison. Encourage your writers to scour their sentences for any unnecessary words, and to change any word that was a lazy choice.

Is there a particular word that keeps recurring that might tell you something about the writer's intention for the story?

Sentences

A simple, clear sentence is a glorious thing. You and your writers can *always* work on a sentence. Find a perfect sentence in the story and celebrate it. Never hesitate to point out a sentence you like. Kids come up with them all the time—absolute drop-dead lines we adult writers would die to have written. You need to listen and look for them, ready to jump in and repeat them in praise. Such a simple thing to do, and such a source of pleasure all the way around: to repeat a wonderful word, sentence, or description that a child has written or uttered.

Once young writers know they are capable of saying or writing terrific lines, work with them on a sentence that isn't entirely clear, one that needs attention. Sometimes working on and improving one sentence is a *fine* thing to have accomplished in a writing session. You can point to this sentence as solid proof of making the story better, one step at a time.

Fixing rogue sentences can involve hours of the most focused and intense revision work and can render the greatest satisfaction. Sometimes I struggle over a tricky sentence for a long time before I finally ask the question, "Can I cut it?" Does it contribute anything to the story, or am I attached to it for other reasons, maybe because I like the way it sounds? I try taking it out to see whether I miss it. Often, I don't.

Sometimes I find sentences in my drafts that aren't entirely clear but seem to be trying to tell me something about the story or character. They hint at something I am not ready to know yet, and I trip over them each time I read my draft. Mystery sentences bear consideration and discussion. Your young writers may need you to ask some questions about those odd sentences you discover in their stories to figure out what's behind them.

Paragraphs

What I like about a paragraph is that it has a shape of its own. Like the larger story of which it is a part, paragraphs have a beginning, a middle, and an ending. As building blocks of a story, they are a fine thing to concentrate on.

As you did with words and sentences, identify a paragraph within your student's story that is a clear and satisfying little unit of information. Consider why it deserves to be separate from the one before it and the one that follows it. Some paragraphs, like some scenes, offer mini-stories within larger stories.

Scenes

You might want to refer to the scenes discussion in Chapter 7. Zooming in on a chosen scene to revise will exercise nearly all the storytelling muscles and, for emerging writers, may be the most important aspect to concentrate on. Try isolating particularly strong or promising scenes, and work on those.

Whether focusing on words, sentences, paragraphs, or scenes, identify a strong example in the draft and set the bar with it, challenging the author to bring *all* the words, sentences, paragraphs, and scenes up to that level.

Chapter 14

One-on-One
Conferences

One-on-one conferences are intimate meetings, each one unique and full of possibility. The more the writer and the responder trust each other, the deeper they'll be able to go. First and always, these meetings are invitations to listen carefully. I've felt kids open like flowers as I've asked a question about their stories-in-progress and then listened intently to their answers. Being listened to: it's pretty irresistible.

Each interaction, no matter how brief, can be tailored to the unique story and writer in front of you, especially if you are open and receptive to the clues offered by the writer and the piece of writing. So much of writing, teaching, and responding to writing involves looking for clues in stories and in the young writers who write them.

I've critiqued many novels-in-progress, working with writers over the course of a semester or within intense workshop settings. I have come to see that being a good editor/teacher depends on being able to read the writer as well as what the writer has written, and being able to assess how much the person can hear. Different responses are called for, depending on where the story and the author are. Learning to intuit exactly where a young writer is in his or her process is another part of our job as teachers, so we know when to stop, when to make a joke, when to sympathize or push. It's a constant juggling act.

Classroom teachers have the privilege of knowing their students, knowing something about how they work, think, and process. This is important information to keep in mind when in conference, especially as we attempt to draw out, challenge, and push toward the next level. Factoring in who you are responding to and respecting that each writer is unique can only be helpful. Who you know your student to be, the vibes you pick up as you interact, what you observe as that writer reads his or her work or talks to you about it—these are all invaluable clues about how to proceed. I never hesitate to deviate from my initial response or way of presenting it if a door opens before me during a conference: a flash of humor I'd never seen before or an offhand comment that introduces a new element into the story. All we're always looking for is a way to have a genuine exchange. Rules and agendas don't matter that much. Sometimes they are good to fall back on, like good manners, when in doubt, but paying close attention to each unique and particular student in the moment of exchange is the best way to go. Flying by the seat of our pants—isn't *that* what so much of teaching is about?

Responding to Stories-in-Progress

Early on, as students make their way into writing their first draft, the most valuable support to give is time, quiet, and repeated sessions to work. To the extent that response is called for, it will probably come through one-on-one check-ins rather than written response and most likely will come in the form of basic questions and expressions of genuine interest and encouragement. I only deviate from that if I sense the writer has no interest or investment in what he or she is writing, or if, over time, the writer is completely unable to get started.

If lack of interest or investment is apparent, then a conversation might tease out possible points of connection between writer and material, perhaps a certain aspect or angle to emphasize. Sometimes a shift to new material is called for.

I've worked with young writers so utterly resistant to writing anything at all that, when sitting and talking with them, I let go of any expectation that they might commit words to paper. Instead I talk with them about any subject they are willing to talk about, and I listen intently for something they say that is clear and clean, a good line. Then I say their own line back to them and tell them it's a good one. I ask whether I can write it down. Sometimes I make a simple story with them, by asking a question that elicits one line and then another that I write down. I am directing, leading, and editing, but they are feeding me the lines. Usually, before too long, I have something I can read back to them. "These are *your* words," I remind them. "You said them. And when I strung them together, they made a story. Listen." When I respectfully read them, the student hears his or her own words, linked together and moving forward, and usually feels pretty good about them. It guarantees nothing, but it's a start. You have to trust yourself about how far you need to go in meeting your students' needs and resistance.

WHEN THINGS DON'T GO WELL,
WHEN THEY GO NOWHERE, OR DOWNHILL

Because it's an intimate exchange, because the writer is vulnerable and exposed, because comments can include criticism as well as praise, one-on-one conferences are ripe for all sorts of dynamics to play out. When things go great—and they often do—it's a joy for everyone. Honestly, though, and despite the best intentions, sometimes they don't.

Things not going well is part of the process—of writing and of teaching writing, too. At least in my experience there is no way around it, only acknowledgment and humble acceptance as you try to make—or simply wait for—things to turn around. Sometimes the writer is not getting anywhere, and there is nothing you can say or do to fix it. You have to wait; the writer has to wait. Do not necessarily stop writing (although maybe that), but simply accept that the process unfolds at its own pace, as long as you keep showing up. I wish I had learned early on to be nice to myself when things weren't going well, in both my writing and my teaching. That's something I still am working on now, and I am fifty-nine.

For students who believe they hate writing and are no good at it, or who struggle with almost every aspect, it will seem like torture. I imagine what it would have been like for me if I had had to draw in school instead of write—to do repeatedly that thing I was convinced I simply had no aptitude for, no ability whatsoever. How miserable I would have been. However, I also think that if I had had the daily chance, and if I had had a true and good teacher, I would have discovered that part of myself that could draw. So the most resistant students are the ones who need us most.

We have to start where each student is and go from there. First, and always, we want to do no harm. And then we need to do *whatever* we can think of to help the writer move forward, which occasionally means doing next to nothing. We have to ask ourselves what works best in each one-on-one relationship, figure out what will help this one writer in his or her development, and do that. One size does not fit all.

Once a teenage girl at a detention center was sent in to work with me after being removed from another class for bad behavior. She was bristling with anger and resentment, and it was clear that giving her an assignment would have been useless, even asking her to write anything she pleased. So I acknowledged that writing might be impossible for her then and there. I told her she could write, or not, as she wanted, and I would use the time to work on a story of my own. Then I genuinely concentrated on my own work, freeing her to write or not write, as she pleased. After a while, she wrote something. I don't know what. The temperature in the room dropped, and the anger cloud dissipated. When it was time for me to go to my next class, I told her I was impressed she was able to get down some words on paper after all. We didn't share what we'd written with each other. I was grateful to have had a moment of connection outside of the consuming anger that she'd entered with. I knew that was as much as I could have hoped for under the circumstances.

Most classroom settings aren't like the ones at that detention center, but that encounter reminds me to consider what can be done in any particular moment. There have been times I've sat with writers and been utterly clueless as to what to say or how to connect, break through, or help, and so I have simply sat in silence—a kind of prayer, I guess.

DREADED STORIES

Stories filled with massacres or maudlin romance, stories that offer a blow-by-blow account of a character's every movement—what's your personal (un)favorite, the kind of story that makes your heart sink? How can you honestly find a way into it?

I've worked with plenty of young writers enthralled by subjects and scenarios that leave me cold. Some write stories that are hard to follow and devoid of plots or characters of interest to me. I struggle to find *my* point of entry into their stories, looking for the single thing I can honestly respond to. Sometimes I simply have to say, "You know, I am really slow in getting stories like this. I need a lot of help and explanation. You are going to have to walk me through it." In asking questions to understand the basic plot—What is at stake? Who is fighting whom? What exactly is happening in this scene?—I inevitably find something that I can hold on to, and I often find the source of interest for the writer, too. "Oh, so this is really about power" (or loss or jealousy or some other underlying concern). Stories that initially make my heart sink can, with basic questioning, become clear and ripe for revision.

STUCK

By *stuck*, I am not referring to writer's block. I'm talking about when I—*and maybe you*—get stuck trying to reach a young writer, when I realize I've been saying the same thing, and it is not getting through. I feel frustrated and even start not to like the young writer so much. Then I need to do what we often suggest writers do when they are stuck: find another way in, around, or through. A waiting period may be called for. First, I can stop doing what *doesn't* work—a variation on do no harm—and then go back to the gate, once again.

Here is something else to consider, and it's not easy: in working with a young writer, both writer and teacher have an investment, and both have an ego. When things really don't go well, I need to think about the role my ego may be playing in the exchange.

Working with writers can be tough. My editor tells me they can be quite difficult! But that doesn't mean we get to be prickly in response, or that we are not players in whatever dynamic develops in a relationship.

Sometimes, especially when I see with absolute clarity what a writer needs to do to make a big leap forward, I can glom on to it in a way that isn't helpful at all. I get pit-bully about it. The fact that I see what needs to be done and that I want the writer to make the leap doesn't mean the writer is ready to do it. It's my job to be patient and keep saying what I see in as many ways as I can, until the writer can see it too, or until the writer lets me see deeper into his or her story or process.

Sometimes I think the writing is hopeless, and then I need to find a way into material, sentences, or even words that I can finally recognize as not hopeless.

Sometimes when I am tired or don't want to repeat myself a thousand times, I get cranky with the story, the writer, or both. It is never right until I come back to a place of respect for the writer and what he or she has written. Hardest of all is when there is no effort or intent on the part of the writer. Why should I spend my time and energy when the writer appears to be unresponsive? We all answer questions like that in our own ways. I think it's because the writer has yet to find the point of connection with the topic, something that makes him or her care about it, and the willingness to address the demands of finding the right words to say it. Finding that point of connection usually entails a conversation of sorts—face to face, through a shared journal, however it can be arranged. Sometimes it's a matter of listening up. I've gained insight into a writer's story by listening carefully to how he or she responds to other stories or to comments made outside of our one-on-one meeting. In my years of writing, I've learned that my stories are with me *all* the time, whether or not I am conscious of them, and so clues can be gleaned at any time. Your students' stories aren't neatly bookended by however many minutes they spend on them in Language Arts or English on a given day. They live on, percolating in the backs of minds, and surfacing in unexpected ways.

If I get too mired down in *what* I am trying to convey and lose sight of the unfolding process, either my own or the writer's, I quickly get sick of it all. I start to wonder just how many times I have made this point on various manuscripts, in lectures, or at conferences. What brings me back is rediscovering how much it matters to these writers that they say what they mean to say, no matter how hard it is for them to try, and how thrilling it is when they break through.

Know *Your* Tendencies

Earlier I advocated for helping your young writers begin to know their own tendencies. It works for us as teachers, too. Sometimes it's worth taking stock of where we are and how we feel about what we're doing. Here are some questions that occurred to me during the time I've been working on this book. See whether any resonate, bear further thought, or perhaps help you see where you need support in teaching writing. What are your own questions?

Why do you teach writing (other than the fact that you have to, it's part of your job)? Do you love it? Do you feel qualified to do so, or like you're skating fast over thin ice? Do you believe writing *can* be taught, and what are your hopes for and expectations of your students (separate from the mandated results called for in your school, district, institution)? How much value do you place on your students' writing? Can you be a good writing teacher and not write yourself? Can you be a good writer and not a good writing teacher? Do you have an image or sense of yourself as a writing teacher that holds you back or gets in the way of your best teaching? How do you find a way to love, tolerate, or relate to the child who drives you nuts? How do you figure out a way to reach the kid who never seems to get it no matter how hard you try? What's the question that you keep buried in your heart, your shame when it comes to teaching writing? Ask it, and begin to think about answers.

None of us got into teaching because it was easy.

Chapter 15

WRITTEN RESPONSES AND LISTENING TO STORIES

Written responses to stories and spoken responses following a reading are two other ways we have to offer feedback and encouragement and to challenge our young writers. We're fortunate to have a variety of ways to respond, and we need to make use of all of them. Writers develop in the same messy, unpredictable, mysterious ways that their stories do. There are no guaranteed moments or methods for getting through to writers with a particular point or suggestion. We never know when that magic click of understanding that moves writers another step forward will happen. Each time we respond—whether in conference, in writing, or following a reading—we have another chance to reach them.

Written Responses

The extent to which you are able to respond in writing, the kind of comments you make, and how you mark up the manuscript will be a function of your schedule, your inclinations, other demands on your time and energy, the size of your class, and your individual circumstances and criteria. How you answer to them is not unlike the writer who must work out how, when, and where to do his or her writing, given life's demands. In both cases, taking stock of what is possible and consciously deciding about how to proceed is the best way to go.

For me, written responses are an important way to reflect on stories. I appreciate that I do this work in private, outside of the moment of one-on-one exchanges. Written responses also turn the table: *we* are called on to write. We must articulate carefully and concisely what we mean to say. I find that my written critiques, more than my one-on-one conversations, impress on me the complicated challenge of writing a good story. A written response helps me identify with the author's hope for a story and address how best to answer it.

In my critiques, I find that, as with my story writing, my thoughts need time to gel. I make marks on the manuscript or a separate piece of paper as I go along, but the added ingredient of time (a day or two) is what usually brings things into perspective for me.

You may not have the luxury of extra time to think about and go back to stories you are critiquing. However, each student's story gives you valuable knowledge about who and where that student is in his or her process—knowledge that will have an effect on your one-on-one conferences and your exchanges in general.

In my written responses, I am guided by my tried-and-true touchstones: saying the story I read, as clearly and concisely as possible; noting the parts of the story that I genuinely responded to with interest, curiosity, or emotion; identifying a chosen number of areas to reconsider in revision.

I usually congratulate writers on how far they have come, whether it's a partial or finished draft or the final revision. Each represents an important step along the way. Something exists that didn't exist before! Writers have a story-in-progress or a finished story they can hold in their hands.

A written response can be the place to reiterate the essential ingredients of storytelling that a young writer has brought together or to say what it leaves you wanting. Whether you write a lot or a little, speak from your heart in words that will be clear to the writer. Be specific about what you like and about how certain parts of the story make you feel. Tell the truth. Make your marks count.

Part of making your marks count is making sure your students know exactly what your marks mean. For instance, I tend to put a squiggly line under words, phrases, or sentences that sound or feel "off" to me as I read along. I tend to put check marks next to words and phrases that work especially well (although I don't do that often enough). In any case, if you are going to put your pen on their stories, they deserve to know exactly what you mean.

TENDENCIES AND TICS, AGAIN

Your written responses are bound to point out some of your tendencies as a teacher, and they're good for you to know. I, for instance, am prone to identify the problem areas of confusion and zoom in on them, intent on getting to the heart of the matter. By doing that, I often neglect to mark the parts that I like and that already work. I tend not to mark the paper until something yanks me out of the unfolding story, so consequently, all my marks appear to be corrections or quibbles. That can be discouraging to a writer. In my separate letter, I am able to address the parts of the story and the writing that work, but I still have to consciously note them on the manuscript. Aware as I am of this tendency, I have yet to conquer it. However, I make a point of telling writers with whom I work that I tend to err on the side of not commenting on story elements I like.

What do *you* tend to do? What aspects of your process might be helpful to share with your students?

In Part I, I spoke about encouraging young writers to flex different writing muscles, not to simply default to their natural strengths. The same holds true for teachers. We at least need to be open to other ways of responding to work and marking papers, and to examining our words of praise, questions, and ways of asking for change. In other words, *our* tics.

If you have the privilege of working with writers over a period of time, they will become accustomed to your shorthand comments. Among my most frequent marginal notations are *tighten; blow-by-blow* (next to a passage where every action is accounted for, simply getting from point A to point B); *emotional response?* (when I've lost track of how the main character is feeling); *just jump in/cut to the chase* (when there's a lot of unnecessary preamble or scene setting before things start to take off); *credibility* (when I am having a hard time believing what I just read). What are your recurring notes? What do you find yourself asking for?

The mark my fiction editor makes when something is both important and completely unclear is "?!". Every time I see it on my returned manuscript my heart sinks because I know I am in for a lot of work in responding to it, but I always know exactly what he means.

Responding to Spelling, Grammar, and Punctuation

If you've read this far, you've probably gathered that I'm hardly a fan of nitpicking punctuation, grammar, or spelling at the expense of the overall development of the story. Yes, spelling, grammar, and punctuation must be addressed (to the extent and at the level it's appropriate for your students), but let's not kid ourselves that addressing them constitutes teaching writing or means that we have done our job in responding fully to a story. Our responses must emphasize content and clarity, with chosen points about punctuation and grammar made *in service* to that content and clarity.

I don't mean to dismiss or discount the mandates you are answerable to, such as teaching lessons and raising tests scores. Stories deserve appropriate spelling, grammar, and punctuation. These skills need to be focused on at various points along the way (certainly before the story is deemed finished). Story writing is a perfect place to teach, learn, and practice good spelling, grammar, and punctuation, because in working with students on their own stories, you are likely to be dealing with text that matters to them, writing they might actually care about perfecting.

I never learned the finer points of punctuating (and my editor and copyeditor would say I never learned them at all) until I became serious about my writing and wanted other people to read it. At that point, it mattered that my words were read exactly as I intended them. I wanted my story to make the best possible impression. And it wasn't until then that I came to value the placement of a comma, the intricacies of quotation marks.

Sometimes, when faced with a story riddled with run-on sentences, I'll read the story back to the writer in a run-on reading.

Invariably, the writer will interject, prompting an exchange that goes something like this:

"No! You have to stop there."

"Oh, you want me to stop? Where? Here? OK, then, I need a sign: put a period."

It's possible that moments like these make more of an impression than an isolated lesson. They certainly would have for me.

Teaching punctuation amid working with students' own words seems like a wonderful opportunity to show the role of grammar and punctuation in creating exactly the story the writer intends.

I also remind kids that even professional writers need an editor, a copyeditor, and a proofreader to whip their stories into shape. No matter how careful I try to be, the proofreader always finds plenty of places where I goofed.

Incorrect punctuation or misspellings show that a piece of writing is not yet finished. Make sure a final proofreading is part of the story-writing process, and have your students seriously attend to this final stage.

Listening to Stories

Reading work aloud is another brave step in a young writer's development. For some writers, an oral presentation is the best part of having written a story. It is an opportunity to shine.

For us, it's a chance to hear a writer's story in his or her own voice—no small thing—and perhaps to find more clues and realize something we missed in reading it silently. It's another opportunity to respond well.

I always find it interesting and revealing to hear an author read his or her own work, with his or her own choice of volume and emphasis. Our job is to listen completely, as hard and as carefully as we're capable of listening. We urge our students to listen to create credible, natural-sounding voices and dialogue in their stories. Authors' readings call on the teacher to focus so that a particular phrase or image or even a chosen word can make a real impression. Sometimes, with practiced discrimination, it's possible to hear the pulse of the story beating. Trust your gut in expressing what impressed you. Say it simply and clearly.

Beware, however, of being seduced by a great reader or put off by a flat one. *How* a story is read makes all the difference in the world, and some writers are better readers than others. Some readers make almost anything sound good. Lines that don't work in a silent reading of the story suddenly come to life and make perfect sense. Listening to a story is one way to take in what a writer has written, but an emerging writer needs you to read his or her work on the page as well. Readings are one way to share and critique stories, but I don't think they should be the only way.

The time, place, setting, and practice you set up for your students to read their stories aloud is up to you and your writers, subject to the schedule and constraints of your classroom and school day. Do what you can. Work with what you've got. The main thing is to create time in which young writers gather comfortably to listen carefully and respond to the stories they hear. You know how long your kids can sit and listen attentively. No one likes readings that go on forever. Develop guidelines with them regarding behavior and manners, and model for them how to give feedback. Set limits that seem to work for everyone and adjust as needed. It's another one-size-does-not-fit-all proposition. I've attended vibrant, fresh, and energetic readings and witnessed others that felt stuck in the mud of ritualized rules and rote responses everyone had clearly become bored with. Evaluate what is and what isn't working with your particular group of writers (because each group varies), and settle on a time and approach that serve the stories and the writers who write them.

No matter what, some days just go better than others.

In Praise of Good Critics and Editors

In addition to listening to the writers, listen for the students who are particularly good at responding to others' stories—the ones who are able to illuminate what has been read. Those students have a precious skill that needs to be acknowledged and praised. Sometimes they are *not* the best writers. I have had brilliant responders in my workshops and classes whose critical insights and ability had not yet translated into the strongest creative writing. But those who are able to listen and respond helpfully to others' work are treasures. Perhaps you have emerging editors and critics in your class as well as emerging writers, and they too should be encouraged.

I have been lucky to know a few real editors in my life. When I was first starting to write short stories, I read A. Scott Berg's biography of Maxwell Perkins, editor of Ernest Hemingway, F. Scott Fitzgerald, and Marjorie Kinnan Rawlings, who wrote *The Yearling*. (The movie about Rawlings, *Cross Creek*, is one I recommend to teachers and students as a revealing portrait of an emerging writer and a wonderful author/editor relationship.) I couldn't believe that people actually existed who did what Perkins did—lived to help writers write the best books they possibly could, who supported and believed in them no matter what. It was like discovering guardian angels existed, and I clearly remember thinking, Oh, I want one of those!

What I've discovered is that editors *are* a rare breed, and they are as wonderful, necessary, and lifesaving as I imagined. They do not want to write writers' stories for them or turn those stories into the books they would have written. They want to help each writer write the best story he or she means to tell. They ask questions and let the writer answer them. They often see into the structure and direction of the story before the writer does, and they know how and when to say what needs to be said. They have their own unique styles, but the good ones have abiding respect both for the work and for the process. The world needs more real editors, so be on the lookout for editors-in-the-making!

Chapter 16

THEIR HEARTS
IN OUR HANDS

$\mathcal{R}$ esponding to someone's story has to be right up there in terms of intimate acts. I am keenly aware of it every time I sit in a workshop, respond to a manuscript, or work one-on-one with a writer. I maintain a fairly high awareness of the potential to harm as well as help whenever I respond to a story. But I am never as aware of that power as when I submit a story to my editor, read a work-in-progress to my writer's group, or stand up in front of an audience to give a reading. Then I remember: this is how vulnerable, exposed, scared, and hopeful my students feel—at any age, at any level of development. I am once again reminded what an act of courage it is to show your writing to others, and I am sorry for any time I have responded in a way that may have missed the mark and hurt or discouraged a fellow writer.

When I worked as a hand bookbinder, one of the consolations my partner and I used to offer each other when we messed up was:

it's only a book. We used to joke about what heart surgeons said to one another on a bad day. But it's not a whole lot different for teachers, is it? These are real people we are working with, listening to, trying to help along. The chances to bruise an ego in formation or stomp on a fledgling hope or dream are scary to contemplate. There is no room for unkindness, thoughtlessness, or condescension as we do our utmost to be honest, demanding, and rigorous. It's a tough balance to strike, and sometimes we make mistakes. Sometimes the hearts we hold in our hands get a little crushed. By us. It's the stuff of 3:00 a.m. horrors. All we can do is keep trying, keep working to offer intelligent, insightful, carefully expressed, honest feedback. That's our job—why we're there, doing what we're doing. They (the writers) have done their part, for better or worse. They have written something. Now the onus is on us, the teachers. How best to respond?

First and always respond with respect. Once that respect is evident (whether in a one-time critique, in a semester-long mentoring program, or built up over months of working with and getting to know a student), I've found there is almost no place you *can't* go with a critique. Respect for the story and the writer has to be established, and here's the *real* kicker: it has to be genuine! I can't just *say* I respect the work, I have to find that place in my heart that knows that the story matters to the writer. I have to acknowledge that it took something for the writer to get down on paper as much as he or she wrote. I have to realize that it represents some stage in that writer's process. When these fundamentals have registered, in close proximity to the part of my heart that writes my own stories, I am ready to proceed.

I have said many hard-to-hear things to writers of all ages over the years. I've asked them to rethink stories they have already worked on long and hard. I have pushed them to dig deeper into their material, suggesting cutting parts that they love the most. Most writers rise to the occasion and return to their work to make their stories stronger.

Every writing teacher and editor knows—or comes to know— that there is no one right way of responding to written work. We deal with distinct, unique writers who are gifted and vulnerable, each in his or her own way. Some need more praise than others; some need nudging, teasing, or no-nonsense clarity. That's our work as teachers: to know what to say, how to say it, and when to say it, gauging how much a writer can take in at any given time. Tone is as essential and tricky in responding to stories as it is in writing them. We can never stop working on it.

The bottom line is that we want to respond honestly and help-fully about a piece of writing. The onus is on us to listen, to focus, and to articulate as clearly as possible the parts that work and the parts that we don't understand or have questions about.

In recent years, I've been teaching a weeklong workshop called the Whole Novel Workshop. Writers send in a complete draft of their novels in advance, and I read and critique them before our week together for one-on-one meetings and revision work. I am always grouchy and then extremely anxious after I've sent out my critiques and before I meet the writers. I rethink the wisdom of such a labor-intensive workshop. I question my sanity for gathering needy novelists all together in one place. I berate myself for taking time away from writing my own book. But here's the truth of the matter, and I come around to it every time, as if it's new. I am scared about holding the hearts of so many writers in my hands, and I know I do. They have sent me their babies. They have entrusted me with their hearts' desire, the thing they care about doing more than almost anything else. They are hopeful, and they have placed their hope in me, in my ability to see into their stories to respond in a way that will help them and help their stories. It's an act of such trust and vulnerability, such an intimate exchange, and until the moment that I finally accept *that's* what's going on, *that's* what's at the bottom of my grouchiness, resistance, and anxiety, I'm a mess. When I stop resisting, though, when I am finally able to embrace how much it all means to them and to me, then we can begin.

Works Cited

Alcott, Louisa May. 1994. *Little Women*. Oxford: Oxford University Press. (Orig. pub. 1868 and 1869.)

Austen, Jane. 2009. *Pride and Prejudice*. New York: Middleton Classics. (Orig. pub. 1813.)

Barks, Carl. 1987. *Uncle Scrooge McDuck: His Life and Times*. Berkeley, CA: Celestial Arts.

Brunhoff, Jean de. 1933. *The Story of Babar, the Little Elephant*. Translated from the French by Merle Haas. New York: Harrison Smith and Robert Haas.

Coman, Carolyn. 1993. *Tell Me Everything*. New York: Farrar, Straus and Giroux.

———. 1995. *What Jamie Saw*. Asheville, NC: Front Street.

———. 1998. *Bee and Jacky*. Asheville, NC: Front Street.

———. 2000. *Many Stones*. Asheville, NC: Front Street.

———. 2004. *The Big House*. Asheville, NC: Front Street.

———. 2007. *Sneaking Suspicions*. Asheville, NC: Front Street.

Coman, Carolyn, and Judy Dater. 1988. *Body and Soul: Ten American Women*. Boston: Hill.

Coman, Carolyn, and Rob Shepperson. 2010. *The Memory Bank*. New York: Scholastic.

Gardner, John. 1984. *The Art of Fiction: Notes of Craft for Young Writers*. New York: Alfred A. Knopf.

Gordon, Caroline. 1957. *How to Read a Novel*. New York: Viking.

Krauss, Ruth, and Maurice Sendak. 1952. *A Hole Is to Dig*. New York: HarperCollins.

Lanes, Selma G. 1993. *The Art of Maurice Sendak*. New York: Harry N. Abrams.

Lewis, C. S. 2000. *The Lion, the Witch and the Wardrobe*. The Chronicles of Narnia. New York: HarperCollins. (Orig. pub. 1950.)

O'Connor, Flannery. 1969. *Mystery and Manners: Occasional Prose*. New York: Farrar, Straus and Giroux.

Potter, Beatrix. 1902. *The Tale of Peter Rabbit*. London: Strangeways.

Price, Reynolds. 1985. *A Palpable God, a Single Meaning: Notes of the Origins and Life of Narrative*. San Francisco: North Point.

Shulevitz, Uri. 1985. *Writing with Pictures: How to Write and Illustrate Children's Books*. New York: Watson-Guptill.

Stevenson, Robert Louis. 1985. *Treasure Island*. Oxford: Oxford University Press. (Orig. pub. 1883.)